GROWING *with* GOD

Published by Paige Tate & Co., an imprint of Blue Star Press
PO Box 8835, Bend, OR 97708
contact@paigetate.com
www.paigetate.com

Design by Chancy Cannon

ISBN: 9781963183139

Printed in Colombia

10 9 8 7 6 5 4 3 2 1

The authorized representative in the EU for product safety and compliance is Authorised Rep Compliance Ltd., Ground Floor, 71 Lower Baggot Street, Dublin D02 P593, Ireland. www.arccompliance.com

GROWING *with* GOD

MONICA STOLTZFUS

Paige Tate & Co.

Contents

Introduction

Have you ever watched a tall, towering tree swaying back and forth in the wind? The branches are bowing, but thanks to the sturdy trunk, this tree is not going to fall. Is the strength only from the trunk or possibly from something deeper that can't be seen? The roots underneath the dirt are the real reason that these tremendous trees can withstand a storm. The roots go deep down into the earth, nourishing and anchoring. The deeper the roots are, the better the tree can grow and thrive.

It isn't only the trees and plants that need a strong root system. We all do! Life can sometimes feel like a storm, with winds pushing us around and rain washing away our foundations. But, if we are anchored by something deep, those storms won't bring us down.

God wants us to grow deeper in our understanding and love of Him. 2 Peter 3:18 tells us, *"...grow in grace and knowledge of our Lord and Savior Jesus Christ"* (New International Version). And who better to do this with than your family? While reading each week's devotion, answering the questions, and working on the activities, you and your loved ones can grow closer together and closer to your loving, heavenly Father. Remember, God doesn't want you to just survive and weather the storms, He wants you to thrive. As you dive into these pages, I pray you will learn how to grow deeply in His love, rooted firmly in His teachings.

"For I can do everything through Christ, who gives me strength."
—Philippians 4:13 (New Living Translation)

Jesus said, "Let the little children come to me, and do not hinder them, for the kingdom of heaven belongs to such as these."

Matthew 19:14 (NIV)

WEEK 1

Walloping Waves *and* God's Grip

What do you love about going to the beach? Ice cream cones piled a mile high? Playing Skee-Ball up at the boardwalk? Building sandcastles day after day? How about jumping in the wild, walloping waves?

It can be so fun to play in the waves. Sometimes, the water is clear and calm, and you can enter slowly without getting smacked and knocked down. Other times, the waves are so powerful and persistent that you must reach out and ask someone to hold your hand so you can safely swim. And when you're being held, and the sea gives its worst, with its swirling, sneaky swells, you still might get knocked down. But the difference is that now, with each whack of a wave, the strong grip holding your hand only gets tighter. You can feel safe amid the troubled waters that surround you.

In life, you may feel like you are in troubled waters at times, but you are never alone. God's strong hand is holding you amid new friendships, cross-country moves, and sports wins and losses. He has been guiding you, leading you, and securing you to Him with each of your ups and downs. As you face them, remember—He loves nothing more than for you to come to Him, reach out, and say, "God, I need you!"

When the troubled waters rise, and you suddenly get smacked by a walloping wave, cling to Him. You are His precious child, and His grip will never, ever let you go.

PRAYER

Dear Heavenly Father,

Thank You for Your strength when I am weak. You never let go, even when the water smacks me down and I have trouble getting back up. Help me rely on You when I am in trouble and know You are always calling out to me, "Come, my precious child."

In Your name we pray,
Amen.

SUGGESTED ACTIVITY | Egg Drop

Grab an egg and collect a small pile of household items, like tape, paper, hand towels, cardboard, bubble wrap, etc. As a family, work together to safely wrap the egg in the materials, creating a protective encasement around the egg. Once you feel the egg has been fully secured, have one family member lift it high and release it, dropping it on the ground. Carefully unwrap it to see if the egg is still intact. (If the egg broke, retry this exercise with a new egg, adding new protective items until you're able to drop it without it breaking.)

Once you're able to drop the egg without it breaking, talk about this as a family: without God, we are like an eggshell, fragile and easily broken. But when we ask God for protective reinforcement, we can give thanks knowing no matter how far we fall down, He will always be there to pick us up again.

DISCUSSION QUESTIONS

Have you ever been hit by a big wave?

What makes you feel safe when you are in the water?

In life, do you ever feel like you've been smacked down by a big, invisible wave? How can you walk more in faith this week, knowing He is always holding you close, especially during these difficult moments?

Now faith is confidence in what we hope for and assurance about what we do not see.

Hebrews 11:1

WEEK 2

Better Than You've Ever *Imagined*

Have you ever had an imaginary friend? Maybe one with a name like Salty, who wears rainbow rainboots and carries an umbrella? Someone who is saved a seat at the kitchen table and comes along in the car and protects you from monsters all night long—with the umbrella! This is quite the friend. And just because other people can't see your imaginary friend doesn't mean they don't exist. You can have the assurance and confidence of what you believe to be there.

One definition of faith is "trusting and believing in something or someone you cannot see." Focus on the first and last words of that definition—*trusting ... cannot see*. It doesn't seem natural to believe in something we can't see or touch, but that is where our faith has the chance to become supernatural.

In Hebrews 11:1, Paul writes to us about the same kind of confidence and assurance in someone else we cannot see. What is he speaking of? Faith. And not faith in an imaginary friend but in our Heavenly Father and His promises. Throughout the chapter of Hebrews 11, Paul refers to Noah, Abraham, Joseph, Moses, Daniel, David, and Samuel—just a few of the biblical forefathers who had incredible mountain-moving, sea-parting, ark-building, giant-defeating stories of supernatural faith.

When you have an imaginary friend, seeing isn't what makes you believe. It's actually the other way around, just as it was for all the faithful heroes long ago—they first believed, and then the miracles followed. What would happen in your life if you closed your eyes to all that is believable and opened your heart to what is "unbelievable"? God is waiting for you to trust in all He says, is, and wants to do for you. And He promises—it will be better than you've ever imagined (11:40).

PRAYER

Dear Heavenly Father,

Thank You for Your presence—always and forever. Help me to know that even when I don't see You, You are here with me, walking next to me all day long. God, I want to have supernatural faith. May my believing lead to seeing.

In Your name we pray,
Amen.

SUGGESTED ACTIVITY | Make God's Eyes

MATERIALS:

Yarn
2 Dowel rods/popsicle sticks/sticks from your yard
Scissors

INSTRUCTIONS:

Tip: Search "God's Eyes" online for a visual of this easy craft.

1. Tie two sticks together in the shape of a cross, using one end of a piece of yarn to secure them.
2. Wind the yarn around the sticks in this pattern: behind, looped around, then to the next stick. Repeat.
3. Change the color of the yarn by tying another piece of yarn in a different color to the first piece of yarn. Pull tightly to secure. Continue the wrapping pattern, repeating with a new color until you reach the size you want.
4. When you are finished, tie the end of the yarn to one of the sticks and snip off any stray tails.
5. As you create these beautiful and unique God's Eyes, remind yourself that God is always with you—no matter where you go.

DISCUSSION QUESTIONS

Do you feel like God is with you always, or just sometimes?

When is it hardest to believe that God is with you?

"For I know the plans I have for you," declares the Lord, "plans to prosper you and not to harm you, plans to give you hope and a future."

Jeremiah 29:11

WEEK 3

Sit Back, Relax, *and* Enjoy the Flight

"Ladies and gentlemen, this is your captain speaking." These are usually the first words you hear directly from the captain after boarding a plane. At this point, you are strapped in with a seatbelt, and you have no control over what happens next. But that is a good thing!

The captain continues speaking across the intercom, giving details about the wind and weather. His or her job is to get you safely to your destination, wherever that may be. Their calm, confident voice calls to the cabin again before liftoff: "Now folks, just sit back, relax, and enjoy the flight."

When we sit down and buckle up, we put our confidence and hope in the hands of our navigator. They have the map and all the directions, and we trust them. We don't have to worry about a thing. What a peaceful trip! However, at this point, we've never seen the pilot. In fact, we have only heard their voice. There are plenty of friendly flight attendants moving about the cabin, handing out pretzels and sodas. But the one in charge, the one guiding us to our next place on the map, has yet to be seen. It is only after we safely land that we get a glimpse of the captain's face as we quickly exit the plane.

The prophet Jeremiah writes of this in chapter 29, verse 11. He tells us that God Himself declares (a strong word!) that He has plans for us—not just any plans, but plans full of hope. We are all travelers, and our courageous Captain holds the future in his hands. He comes over the loudspeaker as we buckle in and comforts us with His perfect trip design. He declares that when we are under His care, we are being lovingly watched over. Even when we hit some turbulence—those little bumps along the way—we can rest assured, knowing He is in control. What amazing places will your Heavenly Father take you? Keep listening to His voice, trust Him with where you're going, and then "sit back, relax, and enjoy the beautiful flight."

PRAYER

Dear Heavenly Father,

Thank You for being my captain. I don't know where I would be without You leading my journey. Help me to relax and enjoy this life, knowing that You are in charge and have great plans for me.

In Your name we pray,
Amen.

SUGGESTED ACTIVITY | Make a Prayer or Bible Verse Paper Airplane

MATERIALS:

Paper (either scrapbook, construction, or printer paper)
Writing supplies (pens, markers, crayons, etc.)

INSTRUCTIONS:

1. Grab a sheet of paper.
2. Write down all or parts of Jeremiah 29:11 (or a special prayer).
3. Fold the paper into an airplane.
4. Line up with your family and send your planes on their first flight. Whose went the furthest? Try it again!

DISCUSSION QUESTIONS

What do you think you are going to be when you grow up?

Where is God leading you this week?

How is God working in your life now to prepare you for His big plans?

This is the day
the Lord has made.
We will rejoice and
be glad in it.

Psalm 118:24 (English Standard Version)

WEEK 4

A Celebration *Every* Day!

How do you celebrate special days? Do you wake up with butterflies in your stomach and a huge smile on your face? Maybe you put on a fun new outfit and eat a pretty cake with your best friends and family. You can do a lot of exciting things to make a special day feel special. But what about the other days? Do you wake up with extra pep in your step? Are you joyful and excited on the non-special days? Well, you should be!

Psalm 118, verse 24 reminds us that *each* day is special: the Lord God made it! And we should "*rejoice and be glad,*" whether it's a Tuesday, a day in March, or raining. That's right! Because God made the super fun days *and* the not-so-fun days. Each one should be celebrated—it's brand new with so many possibilities.

In the movie *Alice in Wonderland*, the goofy characters sit around a long, decorated table and welcome a shy Alice to their "un-birthday party." She is quite confused until they explain that the day is *not* for celebrating anyone's birthday; it's for celebrating everyone's un-birthdays. And Alice joins in the fun, saying with a huge smile, "Why, today is *my* un-birthday too!" And the party continues!

Could you give it a try? Could you wake up tomorrow with the attitude that even though it isn't a holiday, it is still worth rejoicing in? What if you shared that fun feeling with everyone you met? Imagine the gladness you could bring into an ordinary day.

PRAYER

Dear Heavenly Father,

I thank You for the gift of each day. Thank You for the air I breathe, the shoes I wear, and the people I meet. Help me rejoice each morning, no matter the weather, and to be grateful at the day's end for all that You've given us.

In Your name we pray,
Amen.

SUGGESTED ACTIVITY | Make an Ordinary Day Extraordinary

Choose one day this week for your "extraordinary ordinary day" and decide as a family what you will do to make it special. Maybe you throw a dance party in the living room, have breakfast for dinner, or plan a picnic in the park! (Bonus points if you also memorize Psalm 118:24!) Whatever you decide, make sure you start the day—and every day after—with gratitude for God giving you this amazing day.

DISCUSSION QUESTIONS

What is your favorite thing to do on a special day?

What is one thing you can celebrate about today?

When you wake up in a bad mood, how can you remind yourself to think of this verse?

Come, let us sing for joy to the Lord; let us shout aloud to the Rock of our salvation. Let us come before him with thanksgiving and extol him with music and song.

Psalm 95:1–2 (NIV)

WEEK 5

Serenaded *by* Song

Did you know that the word "sing" is used over 400 times throughout the Bible? And fifty of those times, it's used as a commandment—a "must" from above. Now, that does not mean God is demanding you take out that microphone and get to bellowing—it simply highlights the truth and importance of music, song, and praise.

The Book of Psalms is a perfect place to absorb thoughtfully threaded words of beauty. Look again at Psalm 95, verses 1–2, paying attention to the tone of joyfulness and uplifting attitude.

Now read Psalm 98:4: "*Shout for joy to the Lord, all the earth, burst into jubilant song with music.*"

What if the whole Earth burst into worship? What would it be like? Stars twinkling, trees shaking, mountains echoing, oceans crashing, bears roaring, birds chirping, and people singing—it would be a musical marvel. God has done great things for us, so let us praise Him!

My family has always loved listening to music. There isn't a bad mood that a good tune cannot change. If someone wakes up on the wrong side of the bed, we play something jumpy and jolly during breakfast to get the crankies out. If someone's feeling stressed, we throw on a mellow melody from a Disney movie and softly sing along—instant mood change! Most recently, in our house and in our cars, we've been listening to worship music—songs filled with stories about sadness turned to joy and hurt lifted into happiness, all because of God's love. And with a hippity-hoppity beat, who can't get on board with that?

The next time you feel overwhelmed by the world or find it hard to squeeze out a simple smile, try tuning into songs of worship. Start with a toe tap, then a hip wiggle. Throw your arms out with hands waving, then shout for joy and let your heart sing. And if you close your eyes and listen carefully, you'll hear God serenading you back.

PRAYER

Dear Heavenly Father,

I thank You for song and worship—a chance to praise You for all the amazing things You have done. Thank You also for the chance to be with You and listen to Your Word. When I am worried, help me to sing. When I am sad, help me to sing. When I am happy, help me to sing! The stars shine and the birds sing for You, so let me join with them in joyful song.

In Your name we pray,
Amen.

SUGGESTED ACTIVITY | Study a Christian Song

Find a Christian song online and listen to it as a family. Talk about the lyrics and what feelings or words come to mind. After listening to the melody, talk about the message God might want you to take away from the song.

DISCUSSION QUESTIONS

How does music make you feel?

How can you honor God through music?

Can you write down some words or lyrics, channeling your inner thoughts and feelings?

The Lord will fight for you;
you need only to be still.

Exodus 14:14

WEEK 6

From Worrier *to* Warrior

Moses said this quote from Exodus 14:14 to the Israelites as they stood at the very edge of the sandy shores of the Red Sea. The angry Egyptians were racing toward them in chariots, directed by an even angrier Pharaoh. It was looking hopeless. Can you imagine the thumping hearts of God's people? Were they frightened? Worried? Scared? Yes, yes, and yes! They were looking once again to their leader, Moses, to guide them through this troubling time and rescue them. His advice? Reminding the tired people of a God who said He would go to battle for them if they depended on Him (and believed in Him!).

I picture Moses, in the next moments, walking slowly into the Red Sea, looking down at the staff and then up to Heaven. And then, after closing his eyes, talking to God. I bet there were a bunch of questions circling in his head. "What if You don't help us? Will we have to quickly build boats or frantically swim across this sea? Or worse—will we be handed over to our enemies?" But Moses ignored those "what-if worries" and focused on the truth. God had delivered them to this place, and He wouldn't leave them now. So, Moses stretched his hand over the water with every ounce of hope, trust, and faith in his entire body. Deep breath ... one, two, three ... BOOM. A miracle happened.

Because Moses trusted and obeyed, the sea was instantly parted in two, creating a safe path for the Israelites to escape. What an incredible story. And it can be the same for you, too. God wants to be there for you, to fight with you and for you, if you trust in His words and His power.

Is there a "battle" you are fighting? In your head or your heart? At school or in your family? Is there a person, place, or thing causing you to lose sleep at night and wake up dreading the day? Do you feel stuck between worry and fear? That is because you are trying to do this on your own. Don't let the "what ifs" take control of you. God has this battle already won. *So, let go, and let God!* Remember that His "fighting" doesn't always look like what you expect. In fact, many times He is silently, secretly solving things. You may not know what He is doing in this moment, but you can know full well what He has already done. The stories are true. He will fight for you. Just stay still, with quiet confidence. He wants to turn you from a worrier into a *warrior who believes.*

PRAYER

Dear Heavenly Father,

I thank You for the times when You turn me into a warrior. You are always by my side and promise to fight for me if I have trust and believe. Help me hold tight to this promise, especially when it is hard to see what You are up to. May I trust that You will be victorious, no matter the outcome.

In Your name we pray,
Amen.

SUGGESTED ACTIVITY | Release a "Worry" Balloon

Draw a balloon on a piece of paper. Inside the balloon, write a worry. Close your eyes and imagine letting that balloon go, floating all the way up to God. As you close your eyes, say, "I'm letting go and letting God."

DISCUSSION QUESTIONS

What does this Moses story teach you?

What is one "what-if worry" in your life that you can try to let go of and let God do the fighting for you?

What is keeping you from handing over the fight?

In the same way, let your good deeds shine out for all to see, so that everyone will praise your heavenly Father.

Matthew 5:16 (NLT)

WEEK 7

Shine *like* the Son

Have you ever looked up and seen the sun's rays streaming through the clouds? It is so magical! We know the light is there, but observing the rays coming down to the Earth helps us remember its power and source—a spectacular star at the center of our solar system. The sun gives light to everything, and we can feel its warmth on our skin. It provides essential food for trees, plants, and flowers. Did you know that the "moonlight" we see at night is actually light being reflected from the sun? Even the moon can't shine without the sun's power. What a wonderful sun we have!

But there's one better: the Son of man and the Son of God. Jesus is the best and brightest light and the most powerful source of life we could ever have. Because He is the Son of God, He has the ability and strength to do what is impossible for us—heal the sick, raise the dead, part the waters, and calm the storms. And when we rely on His power, Jesus helps us do hard things that seem impossible, like forgiving others, loving our enemies, or doing the right thing when no one else is.

In this verse, Matthew reminds us that when we bring even the smallest bit of light into this dark world through simple good deeds, like cheering up a sad friend, smiling at a stranger, carrying groceries for our parents, or speaking the truth instead of a lie, we are shining like the Son. His glory, greatness, and power reflect off our faces and hearts and spill out into the world. And this world needs much more light from the beautiful "Son-shine" and you.

PRAYER

Dear Heavenly Father,

We thank You for Your incredible power and light. With the sun, the world is brightened from darkness. And with You, our hearts are brightened, too. Help me to reflect Your light and love wherever I go.

In Your name we pray,
Amen.

SUGGESTED ACTIVITY | Shine a Light

Grab a piece of paper, a small flashlight, and a sharpened pencil. Gather in a darkened room and have one family member hold the piece of paper with one hand and shine the flashlight onto the back of the paper with the other. Have the remaining family members face the front side of the paper and gently punch holes in it with the pencil. Do you notice how the light intensifies with every hole that's added? Keep going until the entire paper is full of holes and the light is streaming through the paper. Talk about how even though each hole is small on its own, when it's combined with dozens of other holes—or in this case, good deeds—it can light up the darkness.

DISCUSSION QUESTIONS

Have you ever seen a full moon?

The God of the universe made the sun and stars (and even knows them by name!). And He loves you even more than all the stars combined. How does that make you feel?

What is one small way you can shine light into the world this week? Is there a person, place, or thing that needs brightening?

Brothers and sisters, I do not consider myself yet to have taken hold of it. But one thing I do: Forgetting what is behind and straining toward what is ahead, I press on toward the goal to win the prize for which God has called me heavenward in Christ Jesus.

Philippians 3:13–14 (NIV)

WEEK 8

Falling *into* Peace(s)

Have you ever taken a moment to sit and watch the leaves fall? They float, twist, turn, and get tossed to and fro by the whirling wind before they finally touch down. Does the leaf ever worry about *falling*? If you stop to watch, you will see more and more uniquely colored leaves tumble through the air, dancing delightfully with joyful freedom and then coming to rest peacefully by your feet—they do not seem to fret or fear! Rather, they almost give us the impression of complete surrender to this next step in their journey. Imagine them holding out their little leaf hands and saying, "Yippee!" In fact, it is in the potentially perilous moment of letting go and falling from the tree that we notice their glorious beauty.

In the previous verses from Philippians, Paul is encouraging us to let go of what is behind us and focus on what is ahead. He calls us to "*press on*" toward the goal God has called us for: a never-ending life with Him! Paul wants us to imagine something beautiful and amazing, so he uses the words "*win*" and "*prize*." I'd say, "Yippee" to that! Now, Paul does not say we won't stumble or make mistakes as we make our way toward that Heavenly goal. However, I believe Paul wants us to know that God is with us as we go through life's ups and downs so we can tackle whatever comes next in our journey in *peace*, even when we *fall*.

PRAYER

Dear Heavenly Father,

We thank You for the joy we can experience in our daily lives, knowing You are always with us. Help us to let go and to look onward and upward toward the prize You have waiting for us in Heaven.

In Your name we pray,
Amen.

SUGGESTED ACTIVITY | Make a Leaf Friend

MATERIALS:

Leaves

Paper

Glue

Googly eyes

Crayons

INSTRUCTIONS:

1. Go on a leaf hunt and find a few favorite leaves, either from the ground or a tree.
2. Glue them down onto a piece of paper, add some googly eyes, and draw mouths to turn them into little leaf friends.
3. BONUS: Imagine what they are saying or thinking. Add a speech bubble or create a scene for your little leaf character.

DISCUSSION QUESTIONS

Have you ever won a prize? How did it make you feel?

Can you think of a time when you didn't want to let go of something? Does it help to imagine something greater waiting ahead?

Think of a mistake you've made. Is there a way God turned it into something good?

Carry each other's burdens, and in this way you will fulfill the law of Christ.

Galatians 6:2

WEEK 9

Friendship Can *Lift* You Up

Friends are a gift from above. They are the "family you choose," as a familiar quote says. These beautiful relationships can really help you on your toughest days when you find it hard to get up and carry on.

What makes a good friend? Going back to the "family you choose" idea, let's think of what makes a strong family. Family is loving, caring, faithful, and dedicated. When you need them, they are there for you. They give hugs, wipe tears, cheer you on, and lift you up. This is the kind of friendship that Paul was speaking of in his letter to the Galatians.

Another example of friendship is written about in the second chapter of Mark: A group hears that Jesus is close by, and they have a friend who is paralyzed and cannot walk. These determined and faithful friends navigate busy crowds and lift their friend through the roof of a home where Jesus is preaching. They stop at nothing to help their friend. And their faith in Jesus's healing powers only strengthens their incredible efforts. When Jesus sees their devotion, His response says it all: "*When Jesus saw their faith, he said to the paralyzed man, 'Son, your sins are forgiven'*" (Mark 2:5).

This story of Jesus rewarding the friendship and faith of those close companions should give us hope and encouragement. It tells us that when we are feeling low and can't move, our friends can come to our rescue, carrying us and our heavy burdens. And we can do the same for them. What joy we can feel when we put others' needs before our own and help hold those who aren't strong. We don't have to lift a hurting friend through a roof, but we can make it our goal to be the kind of friend who brightens life up when things are looking down.

PRAYER

Dear Heavenly Father,

Help us to be helpers, to have eyes to see and ears to hear those who need us most. By putting others first, we give You an opportunity to work through us for the greater good. Let us carry, lift, and serve, bringing those around us closer to You, Lord.

In Your name we pray,
Amen.

SUGGESTED ACTIVITY | Friendship Flowers

MATERIALS:

Various colors of paper

Markers/crayons

Scissors

Glue

INSTRUCTIONS:

1. From the different colors of paper, cut out shapes of a flower's parts: a stem, leaves, and petals.
2. Glue them down on a different piece of paper.
3. On each petal, write a word that describes a good friend.
4. BONUS: Write a nice note on the back and give this to a friend.

DISCUSSION QUESTIONS

What did you do for others today?

How can you help someone close to you?

Is there someone in your life with a burden you could help lift? Even someone who is difficult to be friends with? Can you bring this person to God in prayer?

Be completely humble and gentle; be patient, bearing with one another in love.

Ephesians 4:2

WEEK 10

Waiting *Isn't* Easy!

Do you like waiting? It's hard, isn't it? There are a lot of times in life when we need to be patient. When your tummy is grumbling for dinner, you usually have to wait a little bit to eat. If you send someone a letter in the mail, you have to wait days to see if they received it. When you find a toy you like, you may hope you get it months later on your birthday. Waiting isn't easy, but it is necessary.

Can you imagine if you went to the playground and no one waited in line or took turns? There would be craziness everywhere! Children would be climbing all over each other to slide down the slide, swing on the swings, or play on the jungle gym—it would be terrible and no fun at all if no one were patient.

In this verse in Ephesians, Paul is asking us to practice patience with *each other.* He uses words to help us, like "*humble and gentle.*" When we are humble, we remember that we are not the most important person on Earth. Paul finishes the verse with the emotion that triumphs over all the others: "*love.*" So, let's connect the dots. When we need to be more patient, we can think of putting someone else first and what it would look like to love that person. At the playground, why do we take turns and wait in line? Because if you look closely, you can see the joy on someone else's face when *they* are swinging, sliding, and climbing. And that is showing humble, gentle love for your neighbor.

When it gets hard to wait, think of ways you can practice patience—yes, practice! You could count to twenty before gobbling your next meal, giving yourself time to be thankful and appreciate how yummy it smells. You could sing a happy song while sitting in the car at a long red light. You could work on a puzzle—those take a while to finish! And with each of these, take special notice of how wonderful the reward can be—the first delicious bite of food, the exciting "go" from the green light, putting that final missing piece into a difficult puzzle, flying high to the sky on a soaring swing. Sure, waiting isn't easy, but what happens afterward just might be sweet enough to make it worth the wait.

PRAYER

Dear Heavenly Father,

We thank You for the many chances throughout our days to show more patience. Help us to dig deep into the love in our hearts when we find it hard to wait. Remind us that good things can come to those who are patient!

In Your name we pray,
Amen.

SUGGESTED ACTIVITY | Bake Cookies

Gather the ingredients for a cookie recipe and form an "assembly line." Have each family member take turns adding one ingredient at a time. Work your way through all the steps until the cookies are ready to go in the oven.* As you wait for the cookies to bake, talk about how difficult it can be to practice patience, but how rewarding it is when you wait.

* *To make the lesson even trickier, implement a rule that no one can snack on cookie ingredients (like chocolate chips) or leftover cookie dough while you wait!*

DISCUSSION QUESTIONS

What is something you find hard to wait for?

How can you practice having more patience?

Can you think of an example of when you waited for something and the reward was better than expected?

With joy you will draw water from the wells of salvation.

Isaiah 12:3

WEEK 11

Watercoloring *with* God

Mixing things up is just a part of life—our lives are like art palettes, with each color held in by shaped dividers. Homework, family, and playtime are all perfectly and properly placed at first—until things start to overlap and your organized art palette gets unexpectedly pushed, tipped, and tilted. Homework and soccer practice start bumping against each other. You have a birthday party planned for your backyard, but then it rains all day. The colors of life blend and overflow into each other ... bold, bright yellows become infused with browns, blues, and reds. The result? A mixed-up mess. Sometimes, it can be so frustrating that we just want to dump the paint and start over.

On the contrary, things done with God are always worth saving. Have you ever experimented with watercolors? In this particular art form, the beauty is in the blending and flowing. Some of the best and most beautiful colors are created from all the mixing up. The presence of the water moving through the paint and pushing lines and boundaries together is the most important part.

How can we live this out? With Jesus as our Savior (He went to the cross for you and me!), we have the promise of salvation readily available in "*wells,*" as Isaiah writes. Fill your bucket and joyfully draw water from this amazing eternal spring of salvation (John 4:14). Let Him flow through your days!

Life is messy. We will wobble and get jostled and mixed up. But if God is our water, our main source, flowing into all we do, I truly believe the results of our mix-ups and blending will not be messy but rather beautiful beyond our wildest creativity.

PRAYER

Thank You for being my main source, my living water. Without You, my life would not be as colorful and beautiful. Help me lean into the blending that You want to do when I prefer things to be kept separate. You are the ultimate artist, and I trust You.

In Your name we pray,
Amen.

SUGGESTED ACTIVITY | Crumpled Paper Art

MATERIALS:

Watercolors

Water

Paintbrush

White paper

Scissors

INSTRUCTIONS:

1. Cut the paper into quarters.
2. Crumple one quarter into a ball.
3. Choosing one color, paint the outside layer of the crumpled paper.
4. Open the paper all the way up and then crumple it back up again.
5. Choosing a new color, repeat steps 3 and 4 several more times.
6. Open the paper and let it dry. Be amazed at what you created.

DISCUSSION QUESTIONS

When was the last time you made something and threw it away?

What is your favorite color? Is it made from more than one color blended together?

How can you trust God more with His blending this week?

Therefore put on the full armor of God so that when the day of evil comes, you may be able to stand your ground, and after you have done everything, to stand. Stand firm then, with the belt of truth buckled around your waist, with the breastplate of righteousness in place, and with your feet fitted with the readiness that comes from the gospel of peace. In addition to all this, take up the shield of faith, with which you can extinguish all the flaming arrows of the evil one. Take the helmet of salvation and the sword of the Spirit, which is the word of God.

Ephesians 6:13–17

WEEK 12

Time *for* Dress-Up

Do you like playing in the snow? How about making snow angels, throwing snowballs, making snow castles, digging snowy tunnels, and sledding down steep hills? And what do you have to do before you go out? Dress up in all the layers! You need enough layers and protective gear to ensure a safe and warm experience in the winter weather. For example, if there's nothing waterproof on your hands, after one snowball fight, your cold, wet fingers will be screaming.

In this week's verse, Paul is writing to the Ephesians in the hope of preparing them for what they will face and reminding them that they are in constant battle—not with snowballs and snowy, wet weather, but with the sly works of the devil each day. Like the Ephesians, if we are not prepared with the proper protection, the enemy will find our uncovered areas of weakness and win while we've given up and are back inside, getting warm.

First, Paul states that we must put the "*belt of truth*" on our waist—we must know the enemy's lies and counter them with scripture rooted deep in truth. He goes on to tell us to wear the "*breastplate of righteousness*." A breastplate protects the heart, which is where our actions come from. He warns us from leaving this area open to attack and falling into sin. Next, Paul says to fit our feet with the "*readiness*" of "*the gospel*." Always be ready to follow Jesus where He takes you, and spread the good news. We are to "*take up the shield of faith*," "*extinguish all the flaming arrows of the evil one*," and, finally, take on the "*helmet of salvation and the sword of the Spirit*." Those last three are true battle images. Would you face your enemy without a shield, helmet, and sword? Surely not!

Just as loving parents carefully clothe their children so they don't freeze in frosty weather, let us not walk out our own front doors without dressing up in all that our Heavenly Father wants to cover us with. We can use all the help we can get to slay the enemy and take on his daily deception—it's a real battle out there! But with God on our side, we have a guaranteed victory under a glorious general who will always lead us safely home.

PRAYER

Dear Heavenly Father,

Thank You for defending me from the devil's daily threats. Help me to put on the armor You have given me so I am ready for what comes my way. I am not alone in these attacks; please lead me and protect me against anything that would take me from You.

In Your name we pray,
Amen.

SUGGESTED ACTIVITY | Create Tin Foil Shields

MATERIALS:

Cardboard

Markers

Aluminum foil

Scissors

Fork

INSTRUCTIONS:

1. Cut out a shield shape from the cardboard.
2. Cover it with layers of tin foil.
3. Decorate with markers. Use the fork prongs to poke it and make symbols.
4. BONUS: Write "*The Lord is my strength and my shield*" (Psalm 28:7) on your shield.

DISCUSSION QUESTIONS

What would it be like to wear all that armor? How would you feel?

Which part of God's armor do you need to wear more confidently?

Which part of your body needs the most defending, your head or heart?

Which part of your body is ready for battle?

And Jesus grew in wisdom and stature, and in favor with God and man.

Luke 2:52

WEEK 13

Growing *like* Jesus

You do a lot of growing while you're a kid. You eat healthy foods and run and play so that your bones and muscles grow. And then, when you go to the doctor, they check how tall you've gotten since your last visit. You pay attention at school and do your homework, so your knowledge grows. And when your teachers ask you questions, you get to show them how much you've learned. When you show kindness and care for those around you, your compassion grows too.

Now, did you know that you can also grow spiritually? How can you do that? Spiritual growth happens when you spend time with God and get to know Him better. When you pray, you are talking to Him, trusting Him with your problems, and thanking Him for all the good things. As you read the Bible and learn about His love, you come to understand how much He loves you.

It helps to remember that Jesus was once little like you. And He grew "*in wisdom and stature, and in favor with God ...*" What does that mean? It means that He also had questions and wasn't tall enough to put the jar on the top shelf. He was just like you! But He grew—in His decisions, in His learning, in His height, and in His closeness with His Heavenly Father. Each moment of His life was a chance to submit to God's will. With each story He told and hill He climbed, with the help of the Holy Spirit and a loving Heavenly Father, Jesus grew into who God made Him to be. Baby steps, moving forward in little ways—that's how Jesus did it, and you can, too. You can grow like Jesus!

PRAYER

Dear Heavenly Father,

I thank You for this life You've given me. Each day, there are so many ways that I am growing. Help me to remember that even more important than growing tall and strong is growing closer to You every chance I get. Because the more I get to know You, God, the more I understand Your love, Your plans, and Your purpose for me!

In Your name we pray,
Amen.

SUGGESTED ACTIVITY | Create a Faith Tree

MATERIALS:

Two pieces of paper

Scissors

Glue

Drawing utensils

INSTRUCTIONS:

1. On one piece of paper, draw a picture of a tree without leaves.
2. Brainstorm simple ways for each family member to grow their faith, such as nightly prayer, memorizing a Bible verse, or weekly Bible reading.
3. Using your second piece of paper, draw and cut out leaf shapes, writing out one idea inside each leaf.
4. Cut out the leaves and glue them to the branches of the bare tree.
5. Color your artwork as desired, and hang it somewhere visible as a reminder of simple ways you can grow your faith.

DISCUSSION QUESTIONS

What do you think Jesus was like as a child?

How can you grow, like Jesus, closer to God this week?

When you have a question about your life, how can you go to God first, in prayer, and put your faith in His wisdom?

You, God, know my folly; my guilt is not hidden from you.

Psalm 69:5

Hidden like Socks *under* Sweatshirts

It starts with one sock. Then, it's a stained sweatshirt. Next, it's a pair of dirty jeans lying on top of a tattered T-shirt. In a few days, you can't even see the bedroom floor. How does it get this messy? I have a theory: you clean and clean and become a bit crazy about keeping your room tidy and neat ... until the one sock. You walk by it, and you glare at it, all the while muttering to yourself, "It's just a silly old sock ... just one silly old, stinky sock. What harm can it do?" You see, once we've let that one stinky sock remain on our floor for a day or a week, others are sure to follow. Suddenly, the relaxed, "Hey, it's just a sock" voice inside our heads begins to get louder, and we don't take the time to clean up the mess at our feet—small though it might be. Eventually, we can't see the floor. It happens slowly but can get out of control fast.

Sin has a funny way of sneaking up on us, looking like a small, insignificant, single, stinky sock. Then, before we know it, we've gotten in deep and feel like we're stuck in a huge pile of clothes. A little lie to our parents about a test or homework assignment might turn into a bigger lie that we tell at school the next day to our teachers. And if we're not careful, we find ourselves smack dab in the middle of a web of lies, though we never meant to hurt anyone. And what's worse? That deceptive devil, prowling around like a lion, is always right there, whispering and encouraging us not to care or confess. He wants us to stay in the web, the mess, the middle. He wants us to believe our bad choices should stay hidden and that it's too late to fix things. But it's never too late. Not with God.

Psalm 69, verse 5 reminds us that God knows. He sees it all—the good and the bad. He knows when we've gotten ourselves into a pickle, and He wants to help. When we read this verse, it shouldn't worry us that nothing is hidden. It can be quite a relief. God doesn't want us to be burdened and heavy with the weight of our guilt. He welcomes our apologies and loves to forgive us! He wants us to get rid of the clutter and be clean again—to have a fresh start ... from stinky socks, stained sweatshirts, and our sins.

PRAYER

Dear Heavenly Father,

Thank You for conquering sin and death on the cross. I don't need to be ashamed or hide my mistakes from You. You know me, You see me, and You love me, even with all my dirty socks. Help me to ask Your forgiveness for anything I've been keeping hidden deep inside. You've given me a clean start.

In Your name we pray,
Amen.

SUGGESTED ACTIVITY | Play Dominoes

MATERIALS:

Dominoes (If you don't have dominoes handy,
you can also use a few books or boxes of playing cards)

INSTRUCTIONS:

1. Grab a handful of dominoes and create a domino train on a flat surface, carefully standing the dominoes up in a line with the long ends facing up.
2. Once set up, have a family member start the train by pushing the first domino onto the second.
3. Notice how when the dominoes knock each other over, they act just like our small sins—quickly turning into more and creating a "domino effect."

DISCUSSION QUESTIONS

What temptations have you faced this week? Did anything make it hard to follow Jesus?

Are you proud of the choices you made in those moments?

Can you pray in the quiet of your heart for God to cleanse your heart and help you to try to keep those "rooms" free from sin?

Each of you should use whatever gift you have received to serve others, as faithful stewards of God's grace in its various forms.

1 Peter 4:10

WEEK 15

The *Perfect* Presents

Can you think back to a time when you wished you could do something that one of your friends could do? Have you ever wished you had the same talents or "gifts" as someone else? I think everyone has.

So, let's imagine you are at a birthday party, and you are watching a friend open a present. You really want that same present for yourself. And then, on your birthday, you get it—the same gift! And it makes you very happy. But then, at the next party you go to, your friend gets the same gift as you—the same pretty wrapping paper with matching ribbon on the outside and a beautiful gift on the inside. And then, at another party, the same present is received again! It happens again and again! How would you feel watching friend after friend receive the exact same gift as you? Would you feel special? I don't think so!

God has given each of us multiple, unique gifts—*perfect presents*. And our gifts are what make us all so wonderfully different. Remember, God didn't create a world full of boring robots who all look the same on the outside and act the same on the inside. Rather, He carefully made each one of us to do something very special. Don't think for a moment that you've been skipped, looked over, or forgotten. Some of our gifts just take a little longer to unwrap.

Peter is reminding us that when we use our gifts to help God's earthly Kingdom, instead of keeping them hidden, we shine the attention directly on God, the ultimate gift giver. Verse 11 goes on to say, *"If anyone serves, they should do so with the strength God provides, so that in all things God may be praised through Jesus Christ."*

If you ever find yourself feeling jealous at someone else's talents or abilities, stop to truly admire the other person for what they are doing and try to imagine it was a gift given specifically to them from God above. Then remember, *you* are going to do amazing things. Because God needs you in this world—you and your *perfect presents* from above.

PRAYER

Dear Heavenly Father,

I thank You for the very special ways You made me. I thank You that I am not exactly like everyone else. Help me to see all my unique gifts and to use them to help others and point them to You.

In Your name we pray,
Amen.

SUGGESTED ACTIVITY | Taco 'Bout How Awesome You Are

MATERIALS:

Paper

Writing utensil

INSTRUCTIONS:

1. As a family, create a list of the layers that would go in your perfect taco. For example, layer one may be the taco shell, layer two could be your protein, layer three might be lettuce, and so on.
2. Go around the table and take turns listing what you think is awesome about each person, using the imagery of taco layers. For example: Taco shell: "Mom, I think you make the best dinners." Protein: "Dad, you give the best hugs in the morning."
3. Continue through the taco layers, and repeat for each family member. That's a lot of compliments to "taco 'bout!"

DISCUSSION QUESTIONS

What do you wish you could do that someone else can do?

What gifts do you think God has given to you?

How can you use your gifts to bless others?

I have fought the good fight, I have finished the race, I have kept the faith.

2 Timothy 4:7

WEEK 16

You Can Run or Walk —Just *Keep* Moving!

Have you ever watched someone run a race? Or maybe you've run in one yourself. There are races of all kinds, from sprints and long-distance running on a track, to marathons on city streets, to cross-country races going back and forth through the woods. But all these races require you to do something in common—finish.

There are many times within a race when a runner might want to give up. Their body might be tired, they might be falling behind, and the road might be long and full of twists and turns. That bench on the sidelines probably looks really good in those moments. But these runners dig deep, moving past the voice inside their head that's telling them to slow down, come to a complete stop, and say, "I'm done!" They know that they have trained and worked hard to get ready for this event, and part of that preparation is being tough and fighting all the way to the finish line. The most important thing they must do is keep moving forward, no matter how fast or slow.

In 2 Timothy, chapter 4, we read about staying the course and fighting the good fight. Some days, life will feel as if we're running with the wind at our backs—everything will be going very well. On other days, things may go wrong and it may seem hard to keep going. But this is when we need to dig deep and put our trust in Jesus. Paul encourages Timothy (and us!) to not give up because the prize for keeping the faith is never-ending life with Jesus in Heaven. That sounds better than any trophy or medal you could win!

Think of the faces of racers after they cross the finish line and imagine how they feel: exhausted, weary, but with arms raised in victory. What a feeling! Keep putting one foot in front of the other, especially on hard days. Take those twists, turns, hills, and long roads as chances to ask for help from above and show the world what your faith is made of.

PRAYER

Dear Heavenly Father,

We thank You for being on the sidelines of our daily race, cheering us on from Heaven above. When things get tough, You run right next to us, encouraging us to keep moving toward the ultimate prize—life everlasting. Help us dig deep on the tough days and think of heroes like Paul and Timothy, who fought the good fight with faithful footsteps.

In Your name we pray,
Amen.

SUGGESTED ACTIVITY | Family Relay Race

Set up a family relay course—whether it's around the block, around your yard, or a quick jog down the street and back. Make sure to clearly mark the starting point and decide on a goal number of laps for each family member to complete. As each member takes their turn, cheer each other on, providing encouragement to keep going.

If a relay race isn't feasible, try a puzzle relay! Grab a small jigsaw puzzle or download an age-appropriate word search or crossword puzzle, and choose an amount of time for each turn. Take turns completing the puzzle, seeing how quickly you can finish it as a group.

DISCUSSION QUESTIONS

Have you ever run in a race? How did it feel when you finished?

Have there been times in your life when you had to choose if you were going to persevere or quit? What did you choose?

The next time you feel like quitting, how can you remind yourself to dig deep and rely on God?

If the whole body were an eye, how would you hear? Or if your whole body were an ear, how would you smell anything? But our bodies have many parts, and God has put each part just where he wants it. How strange a body would be if it had only one part!

1 Corinthians 12:17–19 (NLT)

WEEK 17

There Are No Small Parts *in* God's Play

Have you ever watched a play at a theater? It is wonderful! There are many moving parts that must work together closely for a show to go well. As the audience, we can see the actors on stage, who speak their memorized lines and act out their parts. But did you know there are many other people working backstage? There is someone working the curtain, opening and closing it throughout the show. There is a group who designed and built the beautiful background scenes and props, and others who move and change them during the show. There are people in the back working the lights and sound so we can see and hear what is going on. Then there are the people who designed and made all the magnificent costumes. Oh, and the writer—someone thought of the idea and created all the actors' lines. Wow, that's a lot of work! It's a good thing there is a big team to work together to make the play a sweet success. If any one of those helpers suddenly decided not to help this big production, the play wouldn't be as great as it could be. Everyone's part is important. There are no small roles, not in a play and certainly not in God's Kingdom.

Just as plays are made of many essential people, the same is true of our families and communities. And He loves it when we work together as a team. When you help your family care for your home and those living in it, you are part of a bigger picture. Helping pick up toys and making your bed is just as important as preparing dinner. So remember, you are very important! No matter what your job is, you are never too small to do God's work.

PRAYER

Dear Heavenly Father,

We thank You for all the ways You knit everything together to work in harmony. My body is a perfect example of many parts joining together and working as one. Help me to do whatever You ask of me, no matter the size of the job, knowing that I am adding to Your Kingdom.

In Your name we pray,
Amen.

SUGGESTED ACTIVITY | Terrific Teamwork

Write down household jobs (they can be fun ones, too!) on pieces of paper and then put them in a container, like a hat or bowl. Write down your family members' names and put them in another container. Have each family member pull out a job and then pull out a family member's name to do the job with that week. Enjoy working together on one important task!

DISCUSSION QUESTIONS

Have you ever felt too small to do something?

What is your least favorite job to do around the house? What is your favorite?

What is one extra way you can contribute to your family, community, and/or church this week?

I am the good shepherd. The good shepherd sacrifices his life for the sheep. A hired hand will run when he sees a wolf coming. He will abandon the sheep because they don't belong to him and he isn't their shepherd. And so the wolf attacks them and scatters the flock. The hired hand runs away because he's working only for the money and doesn't really care about the sheep. I am the good shepherd; I know my own sheep, and they know me, just as my Father knows me, and I know the Father. So I sacrifice my life for the sheep.

John 10:11–15

WEEK 18

Follow *the* Leader

Long ago, shepherds had a very important job, and it was more than just counting sheep. A shepherd's job was to take care of the flock of sheep. That means he fed them, guided them, watched over them, carried them when they were hurt, and most importantly, *protected* them, even if he had to put his own life in danger.

During the day, shepherds led their sheep to graze or eat in green pastures and drink from fresh streams. At night, the shepherds took their sheep to the sheepfold, which is a three-walled "home," to protect the sheep from thieves and wild animals. But the sheepfold did not have a door built into it. Instead, the shepherd kept watch there, with his own body lying down in the opening to keep the sheep from getting out and danger from getting in. Jesus promises to do the same for us in John 10:9–10: "*I am the gate; whoever enters through me will be saved. They will come in and go out and find pasture. The thief comes only to steal and kill and destroy; I have come that they may have life and have it to the full*" (NIV).

Imagine if a wolf came—it would have to get through the shepherd first. And if *you* were a sleepy sheep, wouldn't it make you feel better to see someone strong and loving keeping you safe and sound?

Many different flocks would often spend the night in the same sheepfold. And although a sheep might get mixed in with the others, it would never get lost. Each sheep knew its master's voice and would always come when the shepherd called.

In the Bible, Jesus calls His people "sheep" many times. He is telling us that we need someone to take care of us, lead us, and protect us. Sheep like to follow, and they sometimes go the wrong way and get into trouble by following other sheep. Jesus, as our good shepherd, will lead us to happiness with green pastures and flowing streams. Jesus also knows the dangers that are outside our "sheepfold." He wants to protect us from any harm and be the guarding gate in our lives. And remember—we won't get lost in the big mix because He knows us and truly cares for us. Because we spend time with Him, we know the comforting sound of His voice. We are incredibly safe when we are with Him, so just follow your Leader.

PRAYER

Dear Heavenly Father,

We thank You for always watching over us. Help me know You better each day by spending time with You and trusting You with my life. You love me and will lead me. Let me follow You all the days of my life.

In Your name we pray,
Amen.

SUGGESTED ACTIVITY | Keep Your Sheep

MATERIALS:

Print-outs of sheep

Scissors

Paper

Silverware

INSTRUCTIONS:

1. Cut out the paper sheep and arrange them all over a table.
2. Make a paper fan and a three-door "sheepfold" with your silverware.
3. Moving around the table and creating wind with your paper fan, try to get all your sheep into the sheepfold. See how many each family member can get in one minute.

DISCUSSION QUESTIONS

In the game "Follow the Leader," do you like to follow or lead? How come?

How can you spend more time with Jesus, so you can recognize the sound of His voice?

Is there somewhere that God is leading you? Is it away from the crowd? How could you be brave and trust that He really knows you?

Remember the Sabbath day by keeping it holy. Six days you shall labor and do all your work, but the seventh day is a sabbath to the Lord your God. On it you shall not do any work, neither you, nor your son or daughter, nor your male or female servant, nor your animals, nor any foreigner residing in your towns. For in six days the Lord made the heavens and the earth, the sea, and all that is in them, but he rested on the seventh day. Therefore the Lord blessed the Sabbath day and made it holy.

Exodus 20:8–11

WEEK 19

Rest *and* Recharge

Have you ever gone to use an electronic device only to find it's out of battery, just when you need it the most? Our computers, phones, and other devices need to be plugged in after being used for a while. They need to be recharged. And so do we! We work hard and get tired, too. Our days can be very full. We should take a regular break from daily life so we can get back up to our 100 percent.

How do we recharge and rest? By keeping Sundays (the seventh day and the Sabbath) holy and spending more time with God.

There is no better example than when God created the whole world. First, He created the day and light. On the second day, He created the sky. On the third, He created the Earth, seas, and plants. On the fourth, the sun and the moon. On the fifth, He created the animals of the air and sea. On the sixth day, He created land animals and humans. And on the seventh day, God rested. He had worked very hard for almost a week and deserved a break. Don't you think so? If God rested and tells us we should too—as in the Exodus verses—then we should obey this important commandment.

Choosing to recharge with God and deciding to rest for the upcoming week might mean we have to say "no" to other things. If we commit to all kinds of sports, parties, errands, and other high-energy activities on Sundays, then we might not feel ready for the busy week ahead. In Acts 2:46–47, we read, "*They broke bread in their homes and ate together with glad and sincere hearts, praising God and enjoying the favor of all the people.*" God wants us to press pause, gather together in worship, and fuel up so we can do all the good things He has planned.

Big picture? God loves His people and gave us His commandments to show us what is best. Slowing down on Sundays might be hard at first, but it will lead to our happiness and brighten our week ahead. So, get ready, get set, and recharge ... with God!

PRAYER

Dear Heavenly Father,

Thank You for letting us know that it is okay to rest. You took time after creating our magnificent world, so may we use Your commandment as a gentle reminder to hit the pause button and rest in You.

In Your name we pray,
Amen.

SUGGESTED ACTIVITY | Make a Special Sabbath Meal

On the next Sunday, or Sabbath, bring out the fancy dishes and candles and prepare a good old-fashioned family meal together, connecting back to the Old Testament. As you enjoy the meal together, reflect on how you can start to slow down more on Sundays, turning busy plans and activities into more restful days that honor and celebrate God.

DISCUSSION QUESTIONS

What is your favorite thing to do on Sundays?

How do you keep the Sabbath holy?

What is something you can "unplug" from so that you are more present with God on Sundays?

Jesus answered, "I am the way and the truth and the life. No one comes to the Father except through me."

John 14:6

WEEK 20

I Saw *the* Sign

It's no fun to be lost. Whether you wander and take a wrong turn down a street or don't know where to go next in a maze, it's a bit of a scary feeling, isn't it? What can you do? You can look for a sign. There are signs everywhere, really.

On the road, there are signs that tell you "one way," "do not enter," "caution," "slow down," "bump ahead," and "stop." Do we obey and listen to them? Oh, yes! There are even more signs telling us what street we are on, where to park, what town we are in, and even when there is a railroad track or bridge coming up. Signs let us know where we are and what is up ahead and help get us where we are going.

Did you know that Jesus came to Earth to be our "sign"? He came to point us to Heaven and direct us in the way we should go while we are on these earthly streets. Proverbs 4:25 warns us, *"Let your eyes look straight ahead, fix your gaze directly before you."* And verse 27 goes on to say, *"Do not turn to the right or the left; keep your foot from evil."* When we get distracted and look around us, we sometimes go the wrong way. Thankfully, God sent us His one and only Son to help us focus and bring us to the place where we were meant to be—with Him, forever!

If we listen to Him and use Him as our guide, He will tell us when to turn around and where we should not enter, and He will lead us when we wonder which way we should go. He sees further than we ever could, so His directions can be trusted. Even when we are far away from where we are supposed to be, He can be our inner compass, setting us straight again.

The next time you feel like you're lost in your decisions and don't quite know where to go, look up to Jesus. He will always point the way.

PRAYER

Dear Heavenly Father,

We thank You for the many ways you help us through life. In a world full of "no turn here" signs, You provide a way. You give us signs and point us in the right direction. May we always follow You all the way to Heaven.

In Your name we pray,
Amen.

SUGGESTED ACTIVITY | Guided to Safety

Blindfold a family member and direct them through the house, giving the best directions you can to guide them safely. (Consider introducing new obstacles or moving some of the furniture if you want to make it a little harder!) Ask them how it feels to not be able to see while moving around things. Switch roles and do it again!

DISCUSSION QUESTIONS

Have you ever been lost? How did you find your way back to where you were going?

Do you feel like you can trust God's destination for you?

Jesus replied, "You do not realize now what I am doing, but later you will understand."

John 13:7

WEEK 21

Unfinished Art

Have you ever asked your parents, "Why?" and received the answer, "Because I said so"? It's a common thing parents say. Sometimes, rather than getting a specific answer, we're asked to just trust and obey them.

If you were to walk into an artist's studio while they were creating a piece of art, you might find spattered paint, molded clay, twisted wires, and much more. It might look like a huge mess and cause you to think, "What on earth is this artist doing?" But to the creator, it's exactly what it should be—a work in progress, not quite finished, but far from where it started. You can almost imagine the artist looking at you and saying, "*Trust me.* It will all make sense when it's done."

In John chapter 13, verse 7, it was Maundy Thursday—which is the night before Jesus was crucified and only a few days before He rose again—and Jesus was telling His disciples that they needed to trust Him. He told them that despite all that was going on, all the unknowns, and all their questions, the story would play out as it should. In that moment, the disciples thought things were a mess, unfinished, and they certainly couldn't see the bigger picture. They only saw what was right in front of them. And we often do the same.

As you grow up, you'll ask the question, "Why?" quite a lot. It might be about small things, like why you can't have a cookie before dinner, play in the park by yourself, or go to bed as late as you want. Or it might be about bigger things, like why you suddenly have to change schools or are having trouble with your friends. Often, your parents and your Heavenly Father ask for your trust, even when you don't understand how it's all going to end.

The disciples were in the middle of an unfinished plan, so they had no idea how much their lives (and the lives of everyone else) would change only three days after Jesus had spoken to them. But we do. We know that Jesus knew exactly what He was doing, and it was all part of a very big, very loving, perfect plan. So, the next time you hear the words "Because I said so," may your heart know it's coming from a place of love and is in your best interest. You might be confused now, but "*later you will understand.*" The artist just isn't finished yet.

PRAYER

Dear Heavenly Father,

We thank You for knowing more than we will ever know. Help us to know that, while we may not understand all that happens in our lives, we can take comfort that You are in control and are the ultimate artist, creating masterpieces from our messes. Let us trust You with it all.

In Your name we pray,
Amen.

SUGGESTED ACTIVITY | Group Art

Take a piece of paper and have a family member draw or color for thirty seconds. Then, pass the paper to the next family member and have them continue the drawing for the next thirty seconds. Keep passing the paper around until everyone has had a chance to contribute. Reveal the final artwork and discuss how watching the art take shape can connect you to God's work in your life: although you didn't know what the finished piece would look like, you still trusted that it would turn out well.

DISCUSSION QUESTIONS

Do you like to create art? Do you know what it feels like to have a plan for your art, even if it's not yet clear to everyone else?

How does an artist at work make you think of God?

Is there a mess in your life that you can trust God to create a masterpiece with?

Whoever of you loves life
and desires to see many
good days, keep your
tongue from evil
and your lips from
telling lies.

Psalm 34:12–13

WEEK 22

Stop, Think, and *Tame* That Tongue

Do you know what's easy? Saying mean things and stomping away. Do you know what's hard? Stopping yourself from doing that! Babies usually learn to say "no" before they learn to say "yes." Isn't that funny? Even the youngest person can find it easier to be unfriendly. With all the talking we do, how can we fix this problem? We need to learn to tame our tongues.

Another word for "tame" is "train." Think about training a wild lion. We need to train our wild words to be gentle. This will be hard at first because training means working hard every day to catch those words before they leave our lips. Not only must we catch lies, but we must also trap the wild words that don't show love and kindness to others.

Sometimes, our unkind words reflect the grumpy feelings we have inside of us. Sadly, once they're out, they can make a bit of a mess, just like when you squeeze out too much toothpaste. And just like a tube of toothpaste, we can't take those grumpy, angry words and push them back in. Once they've escaped, they're out for good. We need to tame our hearts as well as our tongues.

So, what should you do if someone is mean to you? The easy thing would be to be mean back. (Hint: the right option isn't the easiest one!) Yes, you've guessed it: the right answer is the harder option, which is to stop, think, and be kind. Remember: "*We love because he first loved us*" (1 John 4:19). Do we always deserve the gentle love God gives us? No, but He gives it to us freely anyway. Let us think of that beautiful truth as we choose our words in our next tough situation. Will our words be wild or gentle? Try to ask yourself, "What would Jesus want me to say?"

PRAYER

Dear Heavenly Father,

We thank You for all the wonderful words You have given us to share. Please help us as we work at trapping the ones that do not spread Your love. Help us to remember the power that words have to build up or tear down. Let us build Your Kingdom with what we say.

In Your name we pray,
Amen.

SUGGESTED ACTIVITY | Toothpaste Test

Grab a cleanable surface, like a plate, and a tube of toothpaste. Take turns squeezing the toothpaste onto the plate while saying something unkind. Then, apologize and see if you can put the toothpaste back into the tube. While you may be able to get some of the toothpaste back in the tube, chances are, there will still be toothpaste on the plate. As a family, talk about how unkind words can be impossible to take back, just like the toothpaste.

DISCUSSION QUESTIONS

Can you think of a time when you felt lifted up by someone's words? How about a time when you were hurt by someone's words?

How can you use gentler words when you talk with others?

Unkind words can stick with someone for a long time. What are some ways you can try to tame your tongue and avoid hurting others?

For where your treasure is,
there your heart will be also.

Luke 12:34

WEEK 23

First Things *First*

If you were to build a sky-high tower with blocks, which blocks would you start with: the biggest ones or the smallest? What would happen if you put the smaller blocks on the bottom and then tried to place the bigger, heavier blocks on top? Your tower would likely topple over quickly. That's because the bigger, heavier blocks need to be on the bottom to support the rest. Then, you can put the smaller blocks on top, building a tower as high as the sky.

Putting things in the right order is very important. Socks come first, then shoes. Sheets and blankets, then pillows on your bed. Cone, ice cream, and then a cherry on top. What if we did all those things backward? Well, when things are mixed up, we can become confused.

We can also get confused when our hearts get things out of order. In this verse from Luke, Luke is reminding us that our hearts are wherever we focus our attention (the things we put first in our lives). But if we put money, clothes, or even toys before everything else, our lives would topple over. We'd be building on a weak foundation, just like a tower built with the smallest blocks on the bottom. So, what (or whom) should we put first in our lives? Who will give us a strong foundation to build upon? You guessed it—God, our Father. And everything else comes after Him.

Luke uses the word "*treasure*" to help us picture something special. A treasure is something we go after with all our might, something we really *want*, like a pirate seeking a treasure chest full of precious jewels. That treasure takes up a lot of time and space in our hearts. So, let us ask ourselves, what is our treasure? What do we put first in our lives?

PRAYER

Dear Heavenly Father,

We thank You for being our treasure. Help us to seek You wholeheartedly, put You first in our lives, and let You be our firm foundation. Everything else can come after.

In Your name we pray,
Amen.

SUGGESTED ACTIVITY | Rocks, Pebbles, and Sand in a Jar

MATERIALS:

Jar

Rocks

Pebbles

Sand (or loose soil)

INSTRUCTIONS:

1. Grab your rocks—these symbolize the most important things in your life.
2. Fill the jar with the rocks. Put the rocks in the jar first to symbolize that the most important things in life should be your focus.
3. Grab your pebbles, which represent the things in your life that should be of medium priority. Add them to the jar, letting them fill in the space around the rocks.
4. Fill the remaining space in the jar with your sand or soil. This represents the least important things in your life.
5. What would have happened if you had put the sand in first? Or the pebbles? Would you have had room for the bigger (more important) rocks? Discuss as a family.

DISCUSSION QUESTIONS

What do you spend a lot of time and energy thinking about?

Is there something or someone you've been prioritizing over God? How can you change your focus this week?

See to it that no one takes you captive through hollow and deceptive philosophy, which depends on human tradition and the elemental spiritual forces of this world rather than on Christ.

Colossians 2:8

WEEK 24

Seeing *the* Truth

How can you spot a lie? A lie is a falsehood, a deceptive idea, the opposite of the truth. Sometimes, the lies we hear are so convincing that they almost sound like the truth. So, how can we tell the difference?

When people study counterfeit (fake) money, they do something very interesting. Instead of focusing on the details of the fake money, they take the time to learn about the real thing. By studying real money under bright lights, they can spot if something is different straight away. If something doesn't look right, their radar goes off, and the truth is revealed.

How can we do the same? By studying God's Word. If we are full of the knowledge that comes from what God says, then when we hear the opposite, a bell rings inside our minds, warning us that we're being led away from the truth. Our radar goes off, and that's the Holy Spirit in action. We can battle each of the lies we encounter by turning to biblical facts and verses, which are thousands of years of God's promises. Let's give it a try.

Lie: You're told you aren't special, not noticed by God, even forgotten among the millions of people on Earth.
Truth: "*Are not two sparrows sold for a penny? Yet not one of them will fall to the ground outside your Father's care. And even the very hairs of your head are all numbered. So don't be afraid; you are worth more than many sparrows*" (Matthew 10:29–31).

Lie: You're told you can't do something hard, and you should give up.
Truth: "*I can do all this through him who gives me strength*" (Philippians 4:13).

Lie: You're told you can't change your bad habits.
Truth: "*Therefore, if anyone is in Christ, he is a new creation. The old has passed away; behold, the new has come*" (2 Corinthians 5:17, ESV).

Now, can you see how there isn't a single lie that God can't bring to light? He has so much to say, so listen up, study hard, and see the truth!

PRAYER

Dear Heavenly Father,

We thank You for Your Word, which is full of truth. Help us to seek You and listen to what You have to say when our internal alarms go off and we think we're hearing lies. Only Your paths will lead us to righteousness and joy.

In Your name we pray,
Amen.

SUGGESTED ACTIVITY | Searching for the Truth

As a family, write down some common lies you may have been told or have believed about yourself. (For example, have you ever been told that you aren't good at something when you really are? Have you ever felt like you've been given more than you can handle?). Search through the Bible (or online) for scripture verses you can use to combat those lies.

DISCUSSION QUESTIONS

How can knowing Bible verses help you when you hear a lie?

What Bible verse can be your "go-to" when you hear a lie in the future?

"Martha, Martha," the Lord answered, "You are worried and upset about many things, but few things are needed—or indeed only one. Mary has chosen what is better, and it will not be taken away from her."

Luke 10:41–42 (NIV)

WEEK 25

The One *and* Only Thing

It's time to go on a trip! Imagine that you're running around your house, grabbing everything you think you'll need to put in your suitcase. Where's your teddy bear and the rest of your stuffed animals? They've got to be somewhere ...

As you're racing around, your mom is trying to tell you what the weather is going to be like while you're away. She says it looks like it might rain, and to remember to pack rain boots. But you're too busy searching for your favorite toys to hear her. So, when you get to the hotel, and everyone else puts on their rain gear to go out for the day, you have no boots, only *bears*, in your bag. Uh-oh—you've spent your time worrying about the wrong things.

In this Bible story, Jesus comes to visit the two sisters, Mary and Martha, and there is much to do. Martha races around the house, cleaning and cooking, making sure everything is perfect for the big day. Meanwhile, her sister Mary chooses to sit at the feet of Jesus, spending time with Him and listening as He speaks. Jesus shares with Martha that she "*is worried and upset about many things, but few things are needed*." He then adds that Mary made the better choice. She stayed, listened, and learned. And that "*will not be taken away from her.*"

Can you relate to Martha? When something big is happening, it's easy to get caught up with the planning and preparation, like running around looking for toys. But being a good listener and staying present in the moment is very important, too. In fact, many times, it's the *only* thing you really need to do.

PRAYER

Dear Heavenly Father,

We thank You for Your presence. You love us, and You want to spend time with us. May we push aside the need to be perfectly planned and ready when all we need is to sit at Your feet and listen.

In Your name we pray,
Amen.

SUGGESTED ACTIVITY | Charades

Decide on an imaginary vacation destination for your family. Grab pens and paper and have each family member draw pictures of things you would need on the vacation. Fold them up and put them in a container, like a bag or hat. Next, have each person draw pictures of things you might be tempted to take on vacation, but don't need. Put them in the container and mix it up. Take turns playing charades with the ideas in the bag, discussing if each item is a want or a need.

Once the game is done, talk more about how this connects with the idea of prioritization. Are there things you tend to prioritize in life, when you really should be spending time with Jesus?

DISCUSSION QUESTIONS

When you're getting ready for a trip, what kinds of things do you feel you need to pack?

Do you ever worry about planning everything perfectly?

The next time you need to prepare for something, how can you be more present instead of worrying about the future?

When he had received the drink, Jesus said, "It is finished." With that, he bowed his head and gave up his spirit.

John 19:30

WEEK 26

Finished *and* Full of Grace

Have you ever been to a library? It's so much fun to check out a book or two (or a whole stack!) and bring them home, cuddle up on the couch, and get lost in the stories. Then, when you're done, you can exchange them for new ones. But what if you lose a book or bring it back late? Well, if that happens, you may need to pay a fee to the library. This is money you owe because you didn't follow the library's rules.

However, some libraries have decided to have a "Grace Day." This is when everyone's debts (or money owed) are completely erased. No matter how many books you've lost or how many days they're late, it's all forgiven. Isn't that an incredible act of kindness? Actually, it's a huge act of *grace*—something given that isn't deserved. The library is taking all the mistakes, broken rules, and money owed from its many borrowers and saying all is forgiven and has been paid for.

Did you know Jesus did that for you and me? He took on all we owe, all our broken rules, and our lost and late things, and He paid for them with His own life. Because each and every one of the things we've done wrong throughout our lives, big and small, has a consequence—a fee to be paid. But God erased them and forgave them when Jesus died on the cross. Do we deserve that kindness, that love? Many days, we don't realize what a huge act of grace that was. Think of grace as God's Riches At Christ's Expense. So, while we're out there losing books and making mistakes, maybe we can stop and take a moment to truly thank Him for all that He has done for us.

The library doesn't wait until the number of debts owed is low or for people to be free from fines. "Grace Day" shows that a lot can be forgiven, and Jesus did the same. He didn't wait until everyone was in a perfect place. Instead, He came when everything was a huge mess, and we really, really needed a Savior. When He said, *"It is finished,"* He was saying He did it *all for us*.

PRAYER

Dear Heavenly Father,

We thank You for paying for our mistakes and messes by giving up Your one and only Son on the cross. When Jesus died for us, it was the ultimate act of love. May we not go a single day without appreciation and sincere gratitude for the grace we have been shown.

In Your name we pray,
Amen.

SUGGESTED ACTIVITY | Throwing Away Our Mistakes

With your family, take turns writing something you've done wrong on a piece of paper. Ask God to forgive you, and then have someone next to you to crumple up the paper and throw it away.

DISCUSSION QUESTIONS

Has anyone ever paid for something you owed?

How does it make you feel when someone tells you they forgive you?

How can you thank God today for sending His Son to take your place and save you?

Everyone then who hears these words of mine and does them will be like a wise man who built his house on the rock. And the rain fell, and the floods came, and the winds blew and beat on that house, but it did not fall, because it had been founded on the rock.

Matthew 7:24–25 (ESV)

WEEK 27

Bring *On* the Winds

In the fairy tale "The Three Little Pigs," the pigs build three houses: one out of straw, one out of sticks, and one out of bricks. Each house takes more time to construct than the one before, with the straw one being the fastest built and the brick one being the slowest. Once finished, the three pigs seek safety from the big bad wolf inside their newly built homes. As the story goes, the wolf goes to each home and tells the pig he will huff and puff and blow their house down. After some huffing and puffing at the straw house, it quickly falls. Then, the wolf moves onto the house made of sticks, and after slightly more huffing and puffing, it also falls fast. At the last house, however, no amount of blowing can make the brick house fall to the ground. In fact, not a single brick is moved. It's rock solid.

In the passage from Matthew, Jesus is telling us that when we listen to God's Word and follow it in our daily lives, it's like building a house on solid ground. So sturdy is this house that when a storm comes, with winds blowing and waters rising, nothing can bring it down.

Further along in the passage is an example of listening but not acting: *"And everyone who hears these words of mine and does not do them will be like a foolish man who built his house on the sand. And the rain fell, and the floods came, and the winds blew and beat against that house, and it fell, and great was the fall of it"* (7:26–27).

Jesus is creatively making the point that not only should we listen to God's Word, but we also need to make a huge effort to do what He tells us. Reading the Bible and then misbehaving isn't exactly what God wants from us. We can be wise or foolish; the choice is ours! "The Three Little Pigs" teaches us a great lesson about working hard so we build a solid foundation: it's all worth it in the end. So, bring on the huffing and puffing and all those winds. Because when we do our best for Jesus, when we build our faith in Him, our houses aren't going anywhere.

PRAYER

Dear Heavenly Father,

We thank You for being our solid foundation. Without You, we would be brought down by the storms of life. You give us guidance and strength with Your Word, and when we follow it daily, there is nothing we can't face.

In Your name we pray,
Amen.

SUGGESTED ACTIVITY | Painting Rocks

MATERIALS:

Smooth rocks

Paint

Paintbrush

INSTRUCTIONS:

1. Think of comforting images, like a cross, flower, heart, or praying hands. You can also think of some kind words or short phrases from Scripture.
2. Paint your comforting image or words on a rock (rocks with smoother surfaces are ideal).
3. Place your rock(s) in your yard or somewhere in your neighborhood to bring cheer and serve as a reminder that God is your rock.

DISCUSSION QUESTIONS

What are some of the "winds" and "storms" in your life?

How can you trust Jesus to be your rock during these times?

What can you do this week to start building the foundation of your faith, making sure your trust in Him is firm?

He will wipe every tear from their eyes. There will be no more death or mourning or crying or pain, for the old order of things has passed away.

Revelation 21:4–5 (NIV)

WEEK 28

No More Boo-Boos, No More *Bandages*

Have you ever fallen and scraped your leg or arm? Maybe bumped your toe or cut your finger? What made it feel better? A big hug? Maybe some ice? Or how about a bandage? There's something amazing about watching your boo-boo get wrapped up with a bandage: the tears stop flowing, you feel safe again, and sometimes, it's almost like the pain has magically gone away.

Did you know that when you cry or feel hurt, God knows and cares? Psalm 56:8 says, "*You keep track of all my sorrows. You have collected all my tears in a bottle. You have recorded each one in your book*" (NLT). Now that's one caring God! Let's imagine that we live in a place where there are no boo-boos—there would be no reason to be sad. That sure sounds amazing! Do you know where this place is? It's where we are united with our Father, up in Heaven. In Revelation 21:4–5, John writes of God wiping every tear from our eyes and everyone living without crying or pain because the "*old order of things has passed away.*" In Heaven, things are different than here on Earth. It might be hard to imagine life any other way, but we've been promised that Heaven is a wonderful place where nothing is wrong and no one is hurt. No more scrapes, cuts, or bruises. And that means no more bandages.

For now, life isn't perfect. We'll continue to fall, get bumped, and need some serious hugs while we walk this Earth. But we can feel a bit better knowing there's something even greater than the magic of a bandage waiting for us: a place where joy, happiness, and healing are overflowing. When we're together with God, everything will be okay. So, dust yourself off, get back up, and try again. Why? Because you've got a boo-boo-free future ahead.

PRAYER

Dear Heavenly Father,

Thank You for Your healing powers. I can only imagine how amazing it will be up in Heaven with You, where there is no crying or sadness. Help me to focus on Your promises when I'm having a bad day, or my heart is hurting. You are counting my tears now and will wipe them away when I meet You.

In Your name we pray,
Amen.

SUGGESTED ACTIVITY | Family Portrait

Grab a piece of paper and drawing materials and create a family "portrait," letting each family member draw themselves into the portrait. Then, either using your drawing materials or fun craft tape, add bandages to each person in the drawing. At the top of the page, write the words "Jesus heals" and place your artwork somewhere central to act as a reminder of God's everlasting promise.

DISCUSSION QUESTIONS

How do you feel when you put on a bandage?

What do you think Heaven will be like?

What do you struggle with on Earth that you look forward to being different in Heaven?

Be strong and courageous.
Do not be afraid or terrified
because of them, for the Lord
your God goes with you; he will
never leave you nor forsake you.

Deuteronomy 31:6 (NIV)

WEEK 29

365 Reasons to *Not* Be Afraid

What are you most afraid of? Buzzing bees with stingers? Falling asleep at night in the dark? Making friends when you go somewhere new? We all have things that scare us—grown-ups and kids alike! But you don't have to feel that way anymore because you have God.

Did you know that fear can overpower faith? When we're scared of something and not feeling very safe, it's because we're walking away from God. But we have the power to control the situation and turn everything around. We can practice walking with God and having more faith than fear. In the Deuteronomy verse, Moses is speaking to God's people, who are afraid (again) on their long journey to the promised land. Although they've encountered many troubles along the way, Moses is reminding them that God never left them, not once. He will not leave you, either.

And here is an incredible fact for us: the words "Do not be afraid" are written 365 times in the Bible. Three hundred and sixty-five! That's the exact number of days in the calendar year. Is that a coincidence? I don't think so! God knows we have days and moments when we're afraid and overwhelmed with worries about everything from monsters to scary movies. But He is telling us that every day of the year, we can remind ourselves of the truth: when we're surrounded by our fears, we can be safe in the knowledge and faith that He is walking with us through it all. With God, even when you're afraid, you can have the courage to be brave—all year long!

PRAYER

Dear Heavenly Father,

We thank You for Your presence in our lives. We thank You for never leaving us, even when we feel surrounded by fear. You promise to walk with us, strengthen us, help us, and comfort us. Let us try to hold on to these verses of hope and power.

In Your name we pray,
Amen.

SUGGESTED ACTIVITY | Faithful Reminders

As a family, look up the following verses. Using pieces of paper or index cards, transcribe all or some of these verses and hang them around the house, letting them serve as daily reminders that we have nothing to fear with God by our side.

1. Isaiah 41:10
2. Joshua 1:9
3. Psalm 23:4
4. Psalm 27:1
5. Psalm 56:3

DISCUSSION QUESTIONS

What makes you feel scared or afraid?

What makes you feel better?

Which of the verses from the suggested activity makes you feel brave?

Is there something in your life that makes you feel scared? Something that you could pray these verses over today and give up to God?

Blessed is the man who trusts
in the Lord, whose trust is the
Lord. He is like a tree planted
by water, that sends out its
roots by the stream, and does
not fear when heat comes, for
its leaves remain green, and
is not anxious in the year of
drought, for it does not cease
to bear fruit.

Jeremiah 17:7–8 (ESV)

WEEK 30

Bloom Where *You're* Planted

Did you know that some flowers bloom in the desert? While most plants need the perfect mixture of sunlight, rich soil, water, and fresh air to thrive, these hot-weather types can survive (and thrive) in extreme heat and dry soil with very little water. So, what cool trick does a cactus have? It stores water inside because there isn't much rain. Isn't that amazing? A cactus is also a very important part of the desert because it's home to many animals, and its long, deep roots keep the dry soil in place. It shows us that if God plants you somewhere for a purpose, He will also help you to grow there.

In our lives, we often encounter difficult situations that challenge us. And what do we usually ask? For that hard thing to go away or to be quickly changed or fixed. But God works a little differently. He wants us to "*grow* through what we *go* through." So, if our difficult times are just taken away or fast-forwarded, we might not have the chance to put down roots and fully rely on God for His guidance and strength.

In the Jeremiah passage, we're told that those who trust in the Lord are like trees planted beside water, sending their important roots down into a stream. These trees don't worry about the heat (just like in the desert) because their leaves will stay green. They don't worry that only a little water falls from the sky (again, like the desert) because they will still have fruit. These trees are thriving with their trust in all God provides.

Do you have tough friendships? Have you been waiting a long time for something? Are you in a new school or neighborhood? Whatever you're going through, God wants you to grow and bloom. He can give you everything you need to do your very best.

PRAYER

Dear Heavenly Father,

We thank You for all that You provide. Even when we're in the middle of a struggle, You give us exactly what we need because You have placed us there. Help us to use the hard times to grow closer to You and bloom.

In Your name we pray,
Amen.

SUGGESTED ACTIVITY | Grow a Plant

MATERIALS:

Small pot with drainage holes (if unavailable, punch a small hole in a plastic cup)

Potting soil

Seeds (Recommended: beans, peas, or leafy vegetables, like lettuce or spinach)

INSTRUCTIONS:

1. Fill your pot with potting soil, leaving a 1-inch gap between the soil and top of the pot.
2. Lightly water the soil and use your finger or a pencil to create a small hole in the soil. (See your seed packet's instructions for the correct depth to plant your seeds.)
3. Place the seeds in the hole and lightly cover them with soil.
4. Water the pot again and place it in a sunny window.
5. Continue to monitor the soil and water it when needed, making sure to keep it moist but not soggy.

DISCUSSION QUESTIONS

Would you like to live in the desert? Why or why not?

When you find something difficult, how do you handle it?

The next time you are given a challenge, can you think of a cactus blooming in the desert? Can you try to remember that God has placed you in this challenge because He needs you there and knows you will thrive with His help?

Rejoice always, pray without ceasing, give thanks in all circumstances; for this is the will of God in Christ Jesus for you.

1 Thessalonians 5:16–18

WEEK 31

Hello, God—It's Me!

Have you ever been told, "Not right now!" or "Just a minute!" You might hear those phrases quite a lot. You might even feel that the people around you are too busy to pay attention to you. It's probably not true, but it still doesn't feel good. Do you know who is never too busy for you? God.

Whenever we want to talk to Him, He is there for us, morning, noon, and night. On the bus, at a soccer game, at the beach—it doesn't matter what you're doing or where you are. God is always with you and ready to listen. Doesn't that make you feel so much better? When you talk to Him, you don't need to use fancy words, sound like a poet, or even make a whole lot of sense. Your heart is what God sees, and He just wants to know what you're feeling—on the good days and the bad.

The verse from 1 Thessalonians says that we should *"pray without ceasing."* Does that mean you should be constantly praying from the minute you wake up to the minute you fall asleep? Not exactly. What it does mean is that you should talk to God as much as you can—and that takes practice. Just like opening up to your parents and friends takes trust, telling God what's in your heart means that you're willing to let Him see your inner self—all your thoughts, hopes, and dreams but also your fears and worries. Remember: He made you, and He cares for you. (And He knows what you're going to say before you even say it!) He wants the kind of relationship where you share things, which involves a lot of talking and listening. That is what will bring you both closer together.

When we pray, let us remember that God isn't an all-magical genie, and we shouldn't ask Him to grant all our wishes. Our prayers may not be answered as we think they should be. Just like when you ask your parents for things and they say "no" or "not yet," our Heavenly Father knows what is best for you. So, you might not always get what you want, but you will always get what you need. Trust Him with your whole heart, and take a moment to say, "Hello!" whenever you can.

PRAYER

Dear Heavenly Father,

Thank You for being up in Heaven, where you constantly watch over us and love us. Help us to believe that You know our needs even before we ask and that You will provide us with what is best. When we pray the same words that Jesus prayed, let us know there is power in them. Your will, Your way.

In Your name we pray,
Amen.

SUGGESTED ACTIVITY | The Lord's Prayer

As a family, read the Lord's Prayer sentence by sentence. Take time to discuss the significance of the words spoken by Jesus:

"This, then, is how you should pray:
'Our Father in heaven,
hallowed be your name,
your kingdom come,
your will be done,
on earth as it is in heaven.
Give us today our daily bread.
And forgive us our debts,
as we also have forgiven our debtors.
And lead us not into temptation,
but deliver us from the evil one.'"

—Matthew 6:9-13 (NIV)

DISCUSSION QUESTIONS

Do you pray every day?

What is your favorite time of day to pray? What comes to mind when you pray to God?

Can you think of a time when God answered one of your prayers?

Is it easier to pray for yourself or for others?

Do you sometimes think of God as a magical genie who is up in Heaven to grant our wishes? How can you change your way of thinking and trust in the message: "*Your will be done*" (Matthew 6:10)?

Jesus Christ is the same
yesterday and today
and forever.

Hebrews 13:8

WEEK 32

Never Changing, Always *and* Forever

Some days, your hair looks amazing, and other days it doesn't. Some days, you feel quick and steady on your feet and like you could run for miles, and other days, you trip up the stairs. Some days, your siblings and friends are nice to you, and other days, they aren't. It's a roller coaster out there! Ups and downs, happy and sad, good and bad—life is unpredictable, and you never know what new challenges each day will bring. In a world that's constantly changing, wouldn't it be nice if there was at least one thing we could count on to remain the same?

Well, there is something that never changes: the Bible tells us that "*Jesus Christ is the same yesterday and today and forever.*" When everything around us is changing, and we don't know what to believe or think, we can rest assured knowing that Jesus remains the same. His character never changes, and He is always dependable. His love for us and His truth remain the same, and we can always count on that. His answer is always, "I choose you." So, no matter what your hair looks like, how fast you are, or who you're having friendship issues with, you can breathe a sigh of relief because Jesus will never change how He feels about you.

PRAYER

Dear Heavenly Father,

We thank You for never changing. Thank You for being the same, always and forever. In a world that is constantly changing, You are someone we can count on. We are so thankful and comforted knowing that You tell us we are chosen every day. Let that beautiful truth settle deep in our hearts.

In Your name we pray,
Amen.

SUGGESTED ACTIVITY | Spot the Difference

Taking turns, have one family member leave the room while the rest of the family changes something in the room. When the family member returns, let them try to figure out what's different. This activity helps show us that although things around us can change daily, even minute by minute, God's love and presence never change.

DISCUSSION QUESTIONS

Can you name something in your life that changes a lot? Do you find these changes difficult?

What do you wish stayed the same every day?

How does knowing that God's character and love will never change help you this week?

Since, then, you have been raised with Christ, set your hearts on things above, where Christ is, seated at the right hand of God. Set your minds on things above, not on earthly things.

Colossians 3:1–2

WEEK 33

Measuring *Up!*

There are many ways to measure things. Rulers measure length and height. Scales measure weight. Our world likes to compare one thing to another, so measuring is what we do. Even people can be measured—not only for their height and weight but also for what they do and how they do it. For example, if you're an athlete, you might be judged on how high you can jump, how far you can throw, or what sports team you're on. If you're a singer, you might be judged on how many tickets you sell at your concerts or the number at which your latest song enters the charts. And if you're a writer, you might be judged on the words that you put down on paper or what kinds of awards you've won.

There seems to be a theme here—lots of "what" and "how" questions that measure ability and skill. These questions are asked of us a lot, and the answers seem to decide how we rank or stack up against the people around us. When we don't measure up, we can feel like we're not worth very much.

But there is another message! It is written in the Book of Colossians: "*... set your hearts on things above, where Christ is ...*" So, we are taught not to seek approval from things like top-ten charts or awards. Instead, we should feel encouraged because God doesn't see earthly things when He looks at us. He doesn't compare us to one another based on how well we can throw, sing, or write. He sees only our hearts and wants us to focus on what He focuses on, which are the things that are above.

It's very hard not to get caught up in what the world tells us is most important. There's a lot of pressure to have fancy things and achieve high status, to name but a few. In truth, it can get even harder as we get older! Each day, God can help us turn our attention away from those temporary things and focus on what really matters, like how much we love Him and what we can do to lead meaningful lives. Remember, the award worth reaching for is the one up in Heaven.

PRAYER

Dear Heavenly Father,

We thank You for seeing us differently from how the rest of the world sees us. Thank You for not measuring our worth the same way other people do. When You came down from Heaven to be with us and took on all our sins, You decided we were worth dying for. Nothing can separate us from that truth. Your love for us is all that matters.

In Your name we pray,
Amen.

SUGGESTED ACTIVITY | Setting Our Hearts on God

As a family, read Philippians 4:8:

*Finally, brothers and sisters, whatever is **true**, whatever is **noble**, whatever is **right**, whatever is **pure**, whatever is **lovely**, whatever is **admirable**—if anything is **excellent** or **praiseworthy**—think about such things.*

Write down the verse, coloring in the bold words. Try to memorize it. Then, going around the table, discuss examples of what Paul is talking about.

DISCUSSION QUESTIONS

Do you want to be famous when you grow up? Why or why not?

What do your friends think is the most important thing to have?

Do you feel pressure to act a certain way, succeed at something, or own something? How can you focus on the "things above" this week?

Blessed are those who keep his statutes and seek him with all their heart—they do no wrong but follow his ways.

Psalm 119:2–3

WEEK 34

Fenced in *Love*

What makes you happy? Is it eating an ice cream on a hot summer's day? Seeing a rainbow after a storm? Flying as high as you can on a swing? Those things are really fun! But does the feeling last? How do you feel when the ice cream is gone, the rainbow has faded, and you leave the playground? Happiness is temporary, a feeling that comes and goes. What God wants for us is a life full of lasting *joy*.

If you ever visit a farm, you will probably see a lot of grassy hills, scattered hay bales, and maybe even a tractor and a big red barn. And you will certainly see lots of animals. What are around those animals? Fences. Why did the farmer build fences around the animals? To keep them safe so that they can live their best lives.

Do you think the animals want to break through those fences to see what else is out there? Let's imagine a farm without any fences, where all the animals roam free, getting into all kinds of trouble and falling into danger. They might wander off, get lost, or be hurt by other animals or cars on a nearby road. It's a good thing those fences are there to keep them safe.

Did you know God protects us with His fences? He gives us commandments and rules so we can enjoy life. Just like a farmer takes care of his animals, God wants to keep us safe too. He doesn't want His beloved children to fall into danger, get lost, or wander off the right path. It's normal to test boundaries and rules. But how do you feel after you've done something that you know you shouldn't have? Pretty miserable, right? Sometimes, the choices that *look* like fun only end up bringing us sadness and heartache. And God knows that! It's exactly why He gives us rules for living and surrounds us with loving fences: to help us to not listen when we are tempted and stop us from making bad choices in the first place.

Joy is found when we obey God, not in a moment when we push boundaries or devour ice cream, because those things don't last. Let us try our very best to keep God's commandments and to live the life we were meant to, with His love keeping us safe in all we do.

PRAYER

Dear Heavenly Father,

Thank You for Your loving boundaries. They keep us safe when we are tempted to seek satisfaction elsewhere. The truth is, only by following You will our hearts be filled with lasting joy.

In Your name we pray,
Amen.

SUGGESTED ACTIVITY | List Your Lasting Joys

As a family, come up with a list of things that bring you temporary happiness. Then, make a list of the things that come from God that bring lasting joy. Put a heart around the things that are lasting and bring you closer to God, and discuss how you can remember these things more often in your daily life.

DISCUSSION QUESTIONS

What things in your life bring you temporary happiness? What things bring you lasting joy?

Why are fences important to have in your yard, at a park, and on a farm?

If you imagined God putting a fence around something in your life to keep you safe, what would it be?

Now on his way to Jerusalem, Jesus traveled along the border between Samaria and Galilee. As he was going into a village, ten men who had leprosy met him. They stood at a distance and called out in a loud voice, "Jesus, Master, have pity on us!" When he saw them, he said, "Go, show yourselves to the priests." And as they went, they were cleansed. One of them, when he saw he was healed, came back, praising God in a loud voice. He threw himself at Jesus' feet and thanked him—and he was a Samaritan. Jesus asked, "Were not all ten cleansed? Where are the other nine? Has no one returned to give praise to God except this foreigner?" Then he said to him, "Rise and go; your faith has made you well."

Luke 17:11–19

WEEK 35

Please *and* Thank You

Have you ever received a thank-you note for something you gave to someone? It feels good knowing that someone enjoyed what you gave them. Have you ever written a thank-you note? Maybe after a big birthday party, for a gift you received? Saying "thank you" is a very polite and kind way of showing gratitude to others.

This Bible story from Luke is about ten sick men who meet Jesus as He enters a village. From a distance, they call out to Him, "*Jesus, Master, have pity on us*," asking to be healed. You can almost hear how much they want and need it. (They could at least have said "please," though!) And Jesus, with compassion, tells the men to go and show themselves to the priests. They get up and obey, but when they arrive, they all realize they were healed along the way. How amazing is that? You would think that they would praise Him, right? However, only *one* of the ten men returns to say "thank you" to their miracle maker.

How does Jesus react? In a very human way, of course. He wonders why the other nine men haven't given their thanks. He healed all of them, yet only one expressed gratitude. Are there times when we receive something—either big or small—and forget to do the polite thing and say, "Thank you"? It might not seem like a big deal to us, but to the person who showed us that kindness, it might mean the world. Being grateful opens the door to so many positive feelings, such as compassion, sympathy, and love. So, the next time someone holds a door open for you or cleans up your mess, or when you realize that God has done something amazing, don't forget to say those two little words. There are blessings all around us; we just need to have the heart to see them.

PRAYER

Dear Heavenly Father,

We thank You for all that You give us. There are so many days when we do not stop to say those two little words to You, even though our lives are filled with blessings. Help us to see them every day and to show gratitude to those around us.

In Your name we pray,
Amen.

SUGGESTED ACTIVITY | "Please and Thank You" Chart

Inspired by the movie *Unsung Hero*, this week's activity is to create a "Please and Thank You" chart. Grab a piece of paper or small poster, some sticky notes, and a writing utensil. At the top of the piece of paper, create two columns: the left side titled "Please," and the right side titled "Thank You." Have each family member write down a prayer request on a sticky note and place them under the "Please" column. Whenever God answers a prayer, move its sticky note to the "Thank You" column. Keep the chart handy so your family can continue to add prayer requests and track answered prayers, encouraging an "attitude of gratitude" for everything God gives you.

DISCUSSION QUESTIONS

Have you ever been sick? How did you feel when you were better?

What is one thing you can thank God for today?

Can you think of something in your life that you have forgotten is a gift from God? Now, praise Him for this gift every day moving forward.

Some trust in chariots and
some in horses, but we
trust in the name of
the Lord our God.

Psalm 20:7

WEEK 36

The Name *above* All Names

As you grow up, you might be given a few nicknames. You might be called "sport" on a day when you have a soccer game. Or "sweetheart" by your mom on your way out the door. Or "bug," "cutie pie," or "big guy." Those are just a few names you might answer to. They may describe something unique about your personality, but all of them are still you.

Did you know that God has many names too? The Bible is filled with the many ways we can call on Him. Sometimes, He is called:

- Abba, which means "Father"
- Alpha and Omega, which means "The Beginning and the End"
- El Shaddai, which means "God Almighty"
- Adonai, which means "Lord Master"
- Immanuel, which means "God with Us"
- Logos, which means "The Word"
- Jehovah, which means "The Self-Existent One"
- El Roi, which means "The God Who Sees"

And there are more! Each one of these names is special and unique to God's character: each tells us more about who He is. He is our Heavenly Father, *Abba*, watching over us day and night. He is the *Alpha and Omega*; He always was and will be the beginning and the end. He is *El Shaddai*, powerful, magnificent, amazing, and almighty. He is *Adonai*, in charge of the universe, the master and creator of all. He is our *Immanuel*, who sent His Son to be with us, so He lives with us everywhere. He is *Logos*, speaking through His prophets; He is the message that we need to hear. He is *Jehovah*, the One who doesn't need anything, yet He still wants us. He can exist on His own, yet He seeks us. He is *El Roi*; He knows more, sees more, loves more, and *is* more than we could ever imagine.

No matter what we are going through, God is all we need. He is everything, in name and beyond. While those around us trust in "*chariots*" and "*horses*," we can put our life in the hands of the One who made it.

PRAYER

Dear Heavenly Father,

We thank You for Your many names. Help us to learn more about You as we say them. In our times of need, may we call on You, not on the things of this world. You are all we need.

In Your name we pray,
Amen.

SUGGESTED ACTIVITY | Celebrating His Name

Write down your favorite name for God using as many art supplies as you want. Then, go around the table and share your artwork with your family, telling them why you chose that name.

DISCUSSION QUESTIONS

Do you have any nicknames?

What does your favorite nickname mean to you?

Can you bring your needs to God this week by using one of His names? How does this help you to trust in Him?

The King will reply, "Truly I tell you, whatever you did for one of the least of these brothers and sisters of mine, you did for me."

Matthew 25:40

WEEK 37

You Did It *to* Me

Do you know that warm, fuzzy feeling you get when you do something good? It's far greater than someone giving you a high five or rewarding your good behavior. It's that tiny spark inside when you secretly spread kindness to others.

That feeling is a sign that you are growing the Kingdom of God. This verse from Matthew states that when Jesus comes again, He will know our hearts by what we did "*for one of the least of these brothers and sisters*." What does that mean, exactly? Jesus explains earlier in the passage:

"*For I was hungry and you gave me something to eat, I was thirsty and you gave me something to drink, I was a stranger and you invited me in, I needed clothes and you clothed me, I was sick and you looked after me, I was in prison and you came to visit me*" (25:35–36).

Jesus is painting a picture of how He sees our actions—when we are good to those in need, we are, in fact, being good to *Him*.

In the story, the people listening to Jesus had trouble understanding the connection. They replied by saying that they never saw Him in need of food, drink, clothing, or help. Jesus is trying to draw their eyes above. Our actions don't just affect those right in front of us—our family, friends, neighbors, and even strangers—our good deeds reach all the way to Heaven.

It's great when our name is written in lights or when people congratulate us with balloons and presents. But do you know what's even better? Doing little things for the people around us, especially those actions that often go unseen. Donating to a shelter, visiting a hospital, making cards for elders in your church, or even just smiling at people on the street are a few ways that we can connect to Jesus every day. As the verse tells us, when you do kind things for others, you are doing them for Jesus, too.

PRAYER

Dear Heavenly Father,

We thank You for that warm, fuzzy feeling that helps us know that we are on the right track. When others just walk by, give us eyes to see and ears to hear those in need around us. Because when we serve them, we are serving You.

In Your name we pray,
Amen.

SUGGESTED ACTIVITY | Doing Good Deeds

Brainstorm a list of good deeds you can do together as a family to bring kindness to your friends, extended family, or community. Once done, choose at least one activity and make a plan to complete it within the next few weeks, remembering that every loving deed we do for others, *we do for Jesus.*

DISCUSSION QUESTIONS

Is there someone in your life that could use your help? Do you have a classmate or friend who seems lonely or sad?

Who is often overlooked in society? Is there a good deed you can do for them?

Do you have any gifts that can be used in your community?

Therefore go and make
disciples of all nations,
baptizing them in the
name of the Father and
of the Son and of the Holy
Spirit, and teaching them
to obey everything I have
commanded you. And surely
I am with you always, to
the very end of the age.

Matthew 28:19–20

WEEK 38

Too *Good* to Hold In!

Imagine you are sitting in a circle with your friends playing the game "telephone." It starts with one friend whispering something into their neighbor's ear. Then, that person leans over and whispers the same words into their neighbor's ear. It goes on and on around the circle until it's back to where it started, and the secret message is announced out loud. You play again, but this time, when the secret message is whispered into your ear, it's just too good to keep quiet. So, you jump up and shout the wonderful news to the whole group. Now, that's not how you play the game, but it's fun to imagine hearing something so great that you just wanted everyone to hear about it right away.

That was the hope Jesus had for His disciples. He gave them a very important job, which was to go out into the world and share the good news of His teachings and resurrection. The word "go" is a command, and Jesus told His closest friends to "make disciples of all nations." Put the two together, and it's clear that He wanted them to get going and tell everyone they met along the way. Just like the game of telephone, the goal was for His important message to be spread far and wide, not just to those living close by.

God asks certain people to share the amazing news of His Son with different countries all over the world. It's how this wonderful message has spread to so many different places and languages. But not everyone is meant to do that. Most of us are called to share Jesus with our family, friends, and neighbors who are right around the corner. It could be someone from school, work, the playground, or a sports camp. Remember, you can also share Jesus with more than just words. Your actions and love show people that something special lives inside of you, and someone watching might want to be like that, too. So get going—this news is just too good to hold in!

PRAYER

Dear Heavenly Father,

We thank You for giving us the important job of sharing Your story with those we meet. Help us to think of the brave disciples who went out and spread the good news far and wide. May we call on Your Holy Spirit for the strength to share Your message and for the words to come to us at the right time.

In Your name we pray,
Amen.

SUGGESTED ACTIVITY | Telephone Game

Go around the table one at a time, and in "telephone" style, whisper one thing Jesus has done for you and why you think His story is called "the good news." It's perfect practice for telling others outside your home one day.

DISCUSSION QUESTIONS

When did you learn about Jesus for the first time?

Have you ever shared the story of Jesus with someone else?

How can you tell someone what Jesus has done for you this week?

He is my loving God and
my fortress, my stronghold
and my deliverer, my shield,
in whom I take refuge,
who subdues peoples
under me.

Psalm 144:2

WEEK 39

The *Ultimate* Fortress

How much fun is it to build a fort made of blankets? You gather up all your blankets, big and small, and begin constructing a huge fort. You search for extra pillows and chip clips and grab some sheets from your parents' bed, along with a few big books and heavy items to help with the build. Then, you tie your sheets to some chairs and prop up the middle with something tall like a stool. After some serious creativity, you've finally finished your secure spot. And it's awesome!

Well, it is until someone shifts a sheet or bumps a book and knocks it all down. Then come the tears and frustration. Wouldn't it be great if there was an indestructible fort you could find shelter under? Where would you ever find such an amazing thing?

Psalm chapter 144, verse 2 tells us where we can find this kind of security—in God. The writer uses words like *"my fortress,"* *"my stronghold,"* *"my deliverer,"* and *"my shield."* These great images of protection give enormous hope to the reader. In the days when this was written, the only way to find true safety was to hide behind a shield or strong wall or within a fortress. Otherwise, you were out in the open and could easily be harmed by your enemies. To imagine God, our Heavenly Father, as our protector, our shield, and our stronghold is a wonderful thing! And this powerful message was written in the Psalms many more times:

- *"The Lord is my rock, my fortress, and my savior; my God is my rock, in whom I find protection. He is my shield, the power that saves me, and my place of safety"* (Psalm 18:2, NLT).
- *"God is our refuge and strength, an ever-present help in trouble"* (Psalm 46:1, NIV).
- *"I will say of the Lord, 'He is my refuge and my fortress; My God, in whom I trust"* (Psalm 91:2).

When it feels like you are under attack from hurtful words or the sting of a sad situation, find refuge, or safety, in God. The blankets and books may fall around you, but God's love and protection will never fall or fail. He is the ultimate fortress, and we're safe when we're with Him.

PRAYER

Dear Heavenly Father,

We thank You for being our strength, our shield, and our fortress. When we need protection, help us not to run to things that will eventually fall but to feel safe and secure when we are with You. Because You are stronger than anything else we could hide behind, and we never have to wonder if You can guard us. You are our loving God.

In Your name we pray,
Amen.

SUGGESTED ACTIVITY | Create a Fort

Have fun and create a family fort! But remember, unlike a fort made from pillows and blankets, God's protection will never fall down or fail you.

DISCUSSION QUESTIONS

What does "fortress" mean?

How does God protect us or shelter us from evil?

What do you need victory over? What are you fighting that you can hand over to God?

He replied, "Because you have so little faith. Truly I tell you, if you have faith as small as a mustard seed, you can say to this mountain, 'Move from here to there,' and it will move. Nothing will be impossible for you."

Matthew 17:20

WEEK 40

Big Things *from* Little Things

Can you think of something that starts very small but grows into something much bigger? A small stick of gum can be blown into a very big bubble. What was once inside an egg can grow to be enormous, like an ostrich. Babies grow up to be adults. And what about a seed? A tiny seed planted in the soil can one day become a flower or even a towering tree.

In this verse from Matthew, Jesus is telling His disciples something incredibly important about faith. He is trying to get their attention by using an earthly example—in this case, a mustard seed. A mustard seed is one of the smallest seeds, yet it can grow up to eight feet tall into a tree-like bush. Jesus is saying that even the tiniest thing can be turned into something big—mountain-moving big, in fact!

The most important thing is not how big your faith is but who you choose to put it in. It doesn't take great faith for great things to happen. That's because it's not about us and what we can do. We just need to get started because that's all God needs to begin. Remember: He has the power, and with Him, "*nothing will be impossible*." We just have to believe that it is possible.

This is great news for you! Why? Because you might feel like you're too small to do anything important. But God uses small things to accomplish much bigger things. Think of David and Goliath! Just like that small shepherd boy facing a giant with only a single rock and sling, if you open your heart and tell God you trust in Him, He will do mighty things for you.

PRAYER

Dear Heavenly Father,

Thank You for taking our small seeds of faith and moving mountains with them. We know how great You are, so help us to weed out our doubts and worries. Let us see the possible instead of the impossible.

In Your name we pray,
Amen.

SUGGESTED ACTIVITY | Turning Sentences into Stories

Create a story as a family! Have one person start by writing down your story's first sentence. Then, go around the table and have each family member add a sentence onto the story. Continue until you feel the story is complete and read it aloud from start to finish. Isn't it amazing that what started as one sentence developed into a much larger, imaginative story?

DISCUSSION QUESTIONS

What is fun about being a child?

Do you think you can do great things? Why or why not?

What would be a mountain-moving act of faith in your life?

Can you think of a situation where you need more faith? What are the doubts keeping your faith smaller than it could be?

Blessed is the one who perseveres under trial because, having stood the test, that person will receive the crown of life that the Lord has promised to those who love him.

James 1:12

Don't Be a *Giver-Upper*

Have you ever tried something but failed miserably? Have you ever had an art project go wrong? Or have you tried to learn how to ride a bike but kept falling off? Maybe you once attempted to bake cookies but burnt them to a crisp. Failure is something we all experience, and it can shape and strengthen us if we let it.

If we stop and look around, we will see that our beautiful world is made of sweet successes, born of people who overcame their fears and failures, people who had a dream and dared to follow it. Their successes didn't happen overnight. Rather, it was their daily decision to stay the course, ignoring the voices that tried to convince them they weren't good enough or it was too hard, that determined their bright future.

A wonderful example of this is Michael Jordan, the basketball superstar. As a young boy, he was cut from his high school basketball team, but he went on to become one of the greatest players the sport has ever seen. How was that even possible? By having a steadfast spirit. He didn't let the words "you can't" define him or stop him from achieving his goals. Whenever we fail to overcome an obstacle, we have that same choice: we can stay down, or we can get up and come back stronger and wiser.

Every time we're met with failure, we must fight the urge to give up. Don't throw away the art supplies, kick the bike and say you'll never ride again, or stay out of the kitchen because you're afraid of failure. We must dig deep and keep on going because it's what Jesus did for us. He faced earthly trials, and His heart and power were tested when the devil threw all he could at Him in the desert (Matthew 4:1–11). During that time, Jesus stood firm on the Word and God's promises while keeping the ultimate goal in mind: our salvation.

For us to succeed, God only needs our trust and cooperation, but it won't always be easy. We will certainly be met with huge obstacles, harsh words, and closed doors along the way. That sneaky devil is going to try his best to tempt you. So, keep your head up, your hands folded, and your heart strong. "*Let us not become weary in doing good, for at the proper time, we will reap a harvest if we do not give up*" (Galatians 6:9).

Don't you think, in the end, it will all be worth getting up and trying again? Remember, don't give up ... because God will never give up on you.

PRAYER

Dear Heavenly Father,

We thank You for supporting us when we fall down. The trials of this world can make us feel defeated, but when we ask for Your help and keep our eyes on You, we can find the strength to get back up again. Let us look to You, Jesus, as an example of perseverance and not becoming weary in doing good so we can press on to that crown of life.

In Your name we pray,
Amen.

SUGGESTED ACTIVITY | Stick with It

Find a large stick outside. Then, grab several pieces of paper and have each person write down a goal they want to accomplish. Attach the pieces of paper to the stick with glue or punch a hole in the paper and tie them to the stick with string. On a new piece of paper, write the phrase "Blessed are those who persevere" and attach it to the top of the stick. Place the stick somewhere visible so it can serve as a reminder to show perseverance and to *stick* with your goals, even when things get tough.

DISCUSSION QUESTIONS

Why do you think it's important to keep going even when things are hard?

Can you think of a time when you didn't give up? How did it feel? What did you learn?

Has there been a time when you quit something? How did it feel? Do you wish you had stuck with it? The next time you find something tough, how can God help you?

But the Holy Spirit produces this kind of fruit in our lives: love, joy, peace, patience, kindness, goodness, faithfulness, gentleness, and self-control. There is no law against these things!

Galatians 5:22–23 (NLT)

WEEK 42

From the *Inside* Out

What do you do when you are getting ready to head back to school? You grab your supplies, of course! You need lots of things to help you succeed in your new grade and classroom. Let's see—you may need glue sticks, pencils, erasers, notebooks, folders, crayons, markers, scissors, and a backpack to hold everything in. You can't do your schoolwork and homework well without the right equipment. But now you're ready!

Those new supplies will get you through the beginning of the school year and maybe into winter. But by that point, you'll probably have to head back to the store to replace a few things. The glue sticks may have run out, the pencils may be stubby or broken, and you may have filled all your notebooks. It's a good thing you can always get more. Did you know that we need supplies for our hearts, too? But you won't find them at your local store. You get them directly from the Holy Spirit.

These supplies are listed in the Galatians verses from chapter 5, and they help us in our everyday lives. We can't do much without a little *"love, joy, peace, patience, kindness, goodness, faithfulness, gentleness, and self-control."* Just as scissors and glue are incredibly important for a cut-and-paste project in science class, so too are the patience and self-control that help us to complete the project. And we need those qualities even after we leave the classroom. Is someone giving you trouble on the playground again? You need to ask for some more kindness. Or is the bus late picking you up at the end of the school day? You could definitely use more patience and joy. Wherever we go, whatever we are going *through*, the Holy Spirit is ready to give us these fruits—these important tools—to thrive within our daily relationships and lives.

And do you know what else is great? Just as you can go to the store for more school supplies, you can ask the Holy Spirit for more fruit to nourish you from the inside out. When you are running low on one of these heart supplies, simply pray and ask for more. Then, you'll be recharged and ready for whatever comes your way.

PRAYER

Dear Heavenly Father,

We thank You for giving us Your Spirit and filling us with what we need. Help us to know that we can ask for more of these fruits by coming to You in prayer. We will be nourished and filled for each day.

In Your name we pray,
Amen.

SUGGESTED ACTIVITY | Fruits of the Spirit

Each family member picks one or two fruits of the Holy Spirit to draw and/or color. Once done, cut out the fruits and glue them onto a larger piece of paper. Then, share with your family how these fruits of the Spirit have helped in a difficult situation.

DISCUSSION QUESTIONS

Which fruit of the Spirit is your favorite? Why?

Why do people need the fruits of the Spirit?

Which fruits of the Spirit do you have in abundance? Which ones do you need more of?

"For my thoughts are not your thoughts, neither are your ways my ways," declares the Lord. "As the heavens are higher than the earth, so are my ways higher than your ways and my thoughts than your thoughts."

Isaiah 55:8–9 (NIV)

WEEK 43

A Crazy Kind *of* Wonderful

Did you know that God asked Noah to build an ark in the middle of the desert, where it never rains? Did you also know that Noah was a farmer and not a carpenter? That sounds crazy, right?

God asked Joshua to tell the Israelites to march around Jericho, a strongly fortified city, for six days and, on the seventh day, to march around the city seven times with all the priests blowing trumpets. Then, after the trumpet blast, the army was to give a loud shout, at which point the walls of the city would collapse. Now, if that doesn't sound like an absurd plan, what does?

Also, while Moses was very comfortable in his new family life in the desert, God told him to go back to Egypt, the country he had fled from. God wanted him to deliver a message to Pharaoh to release His people, or else there would be many plagues set upon them.

God also told Abraham, at the age of one hundred, that he would have a son and would be the father to nations more numerous than the stars in the sky.

These are just some of the stories we can find in the Bible in which God relays a curious message. But it's never without reason. He always has a plan, and sometimes, part of that plan is just to listen and be open to crazy ideas. Sometimes, the strangest things can turn into the most amazing victories, and we could be asked to be a part of it.

What comfort can we find in a crazy quest from God? First, count it as a privilege; we are in good company! Second, He only needs our trust and obedience, no matter how foolish it may seem to the world, and He will do the rest. It's also important to remember that when God calls you to do something for Him that might seem a little crazy, it might not be what you think. It may seem like a bad idea, but since our Heavenly Father is outside of time and space, His thoughts are not our thoughts, and His ways are not our ways. He can use all things for good, no matter what it might look like to you now. Some may call it crazy, but we can call it wonderful.

PRAYER

Dear Heavenly Father,

We thank You for having higher thoughts and higher ways. Our human minds and abilities can only get us so far, but with Your infinite power, You can do all things. When You ask us to do something we consider crazy, help us to trust and obey.

In Your name we pray,
Amen.

SUGGESTED ACTIVITY | His Thoughts and Ways

Sketch an outdoor scene, including the ground and the sky in your drawing. Write the words "my thoughts and my ways" on the ground, and the words "God's thoughts and God's ways" up in the sky. Use markers, colored pencils, or other drawing materials to add lots of color and bring your artwork to life!

DISCUSSION QUESTIONS

What might God ask you to do that, at first, seems crazy?

How can you trust God about something you don't quite understand?

For we are God's masterpiece. He has created us anew in Christ Jesus, so that we can do the good things he planned for us long ago.

Ephesians 2:10 (NLT)

WEEK 44

An Audience of *One*

Have you ever felt like you didn't fit in? Have you ever focused on all the ways you are different than everyone around you? Well, that isn't how God wants you to feel. He wants you to know you were created perfectly and wonderfully for a reason. You don't need to prove yourself to others or look for them to like you and accept you to feel loved.

This idea is illustrated incredibly well in Max Lucado's beautiful picture book *You Are Special*. The characters in the book are called Wemmicks and look like wooden puppets. They walk around and give stickers to one another based only on things they can see on the outside. They give gold stars to those who look beautiful and have a lot of talent, and they give gray dots to those who have bumps and bruises and aren't good at anything. It almost sounds a little like our world, doesn't it?

The story's main character, Punchinello, has many nicks and scratches, and he doesn't have an amazing talent. He is covered in many gray dots, so he walks around feeling very defeated until one day, he meets a Wemmick who has no stickers on her. The other Wemmicks try to put stickers on her, but they just won't stick. When Punchinello asks how that is possible, she explains that the stickers don't stick because they don't matter to her or to the one who created her. She is completely unaffected by what others think or say about her. Instead, her worth comes from spending each day with her wonderful and loving creator, the woodcarver.

What a lovely story to bring to life the way your creator feels about you. There are lots of messages—or stickers—that people will try to give you in the hope that they stick. Some of these messages will affect how you see yourself in the mirror and make you doubt how you think you should be treated. The only message you need to listen to is from God. He is the only one that matters. When you realize this, nothing can stick to you, and you'll discover that you aren't bothered by what others think. You'll finally be free to live how you were born to be—*His masterpiece*.

PRAYER

Dear Heavenly Father,

We thank You for creating us as Your masterpiece. The more time we spend with You, the more we realize our worth is found in You, not in the way others see us. May the stickers and labels of the world just fall to the ground while we walk with You.

In Your name we pray,
Amen.

SUGGESTED ACTIVITY | Still Worth It!

Bring a $1/$5/$10 bill to the table (if one is available). Crumple it up and ask how much it's worth now that it's crumpled. Does anyone still want it? Of course! Even though it's creased, it still holds value. How is this similar to the way God sees us?

DISCUSSION QUESTIONS

Why are we called God's masterpiece?

Can you think of any labels that people try to stick on us? How are they earned or taken away?

How can you listen more to what God says about you this week?

"So he got up and went to his father. But while he was still a long way off, his father saw him and was filled with compassion for him; he ran to his son, threw his arms around him and kissed him. The son said to him, 'Father, I have sinned against heaven and against you. I am no longer worthy to be called your son.' But the father said to his servants, 'Quick! Bring the best robe and put it on him. Put a ring on his finger and sandals on his feet. Bring the fattened calf and kill it. Let's have a feast and celebrate. For this son of mine was dead and is alive again; he was lost and is found.' So they began to celebrate."

Luke 15:20–24 (NIV)

WEEK 45

A Big Hug *and* a Huge Party

Have you ever felt like you had done something so wrong that you couldn't be forgiven? That your decisions had taken you too far away from God and your loved ones, and maybe things just couldn't be fixed? Well, let us look to scripture to see if that's true.

In the Bible verses from Luke, Jesus is telling a story to show His listeners just how much the Father loves us. A son asks his father for his inheritance or money set aside for him (which is a bit rude since his parents are still alive!). Then, he takes the money, leaves his family, and spends it all on silly things. When he realizes his mistake, the son has an important decision to make—does he stay away from his father and keep making mistakes, or does he go back to his father and admit he was wrong?

There are so many wonderful parts to this story, the first being that the son does come back. He may have made some bad choices, but in the end, his heart led him back to his father. Second, when the father sees his son, he runs to him and gives him a big hug. What once separated them is over, and they are together again. The son does something very important to heal their relationship—he admits he was wrong. And because of this, he receives an abundance of forgiveness. So much, in fact, that the father rejoices and throws his son a big welcome home party.

The story that Jesus tells can bring us so much joy and comfort in our daily lives. We are going to make a lot of mistakes, and some of those will feel like they've taken us away from God. But He is never too far away. He rejoices when our hearts turn back to Him and we say we are sorry. His forgiveness is always there for us, waiting. So come back to Him, for He is waiting for you with open arms. Be ready to receive that big hug and celebrate with a huge party.

PRAYER

Dear Heavenly Father,

We thank You for Your never-ending forgiveness. We often stray, thinking we can find something better than what You can offer us. Help us to stay close to You. When we make mistakes, help us to turn our hearts back to You, admit our wrongs, and accept Your gracious gift of new beginnings.

In Your name we pray,
Amen.

SUGGESTED ACTIVITY | Family Skit

Act out the following scenes from Luke 15:

* The son asking his father for his inheritance
* The son leaving home and spending all the money
* The son feeling hungry and living with pigs
* The son returning home, and his father running to greet him
* The son saying sorry to his father
* A huge celebration

DISCUSSION QUESTIONS

What did the son do wrong?

How did the father react when he saw his son again?

How is the father's reaction just like God's love for us?

Have you ever felt like the son in this story? How can this story of forgiveness bring you comfort and healing?

And if the Spirit of him who raised Jesus from the dead is living in you, he who raised Christ from the dead will also give life to your mortal bodies because of his Spirit who lives in you.

Romans 8:11

WEEK 46

A Superhero *in* Sneakers

Wouldn't it be awesome to be a superhero? What special power would you wish for? Maybe you would want to be able to fly, stretch your body, teleport to another place, or make yourself invisible. To be a regular person one minute and then, in a flash, be able to do something amazing is what childhood dreams are made of.

What if I told you that you already have superpowers inside of you? Because you do! In the verse from Romans, Paul is telling the Romans that God's Spirit lives in those who believe He raised Jesus from the dead. (What a cool superpower to have!) And we are given that same Spirit with resurrection power! Is there anything more powerful?

Because Jesus lives, we have access to an incredible life—one where we don't have to rely on our own abilities anymore. The tough days, the uphill battles, the losses, and the storms—we have been given all we need to survive and thrive through it all. Think of Clark Kent and Superman or Peter Parker and Spiderman. When those superheroes are undercover, they only have human strength. But when they decide to unleash their superpowers, they can achieve anything. How different would comic books and movies be if those characters had never become superheroes and discovered all they were capable of?

It's the same with us—we are meant for so much more—except we don't have to worry about doing it alone. Our Heavenly Father knows that we need help, and that's why He sent His Son to save us and His Holy Spirit to remain in us. In 2 Timothy 1:7, we read, *"For the Spirit God gave us does not make us timid, but gives us power, love and self-discipline."* We are not supposed to be timid or scared. Instead, we are meant to be confident and full of life-giving power.

So, the next time you're faced with a challenge and are tempted to say, "I can't," remember that you can. Just grab your cape, call on the Holy Spirit, and give yourself a cool name because you're a superhero in sneakers.

PRAYER

Dear Heavenly Father,

We thank You for giving us our superpower. There are so many days when it's hard to face our troubles, but we have so much more to show this world. Help us to call on the Holy Spirit when we hear the words "I can't" echo in our minds and hearts. The truth is that we can because we have You.

In Your name we pray,
Amen.

SUGGESTED ACTIVITY | Make Superhero Masks

Grab string, scissors, coloring materials, and a paper plate for each family member. Carefully cut out holes in the paper plate for your eyes, mouth, and/or nose, and punch small holes in the sides for the string. Decide on your superhero name and decorate the outside of your paper plate to fit your superhero character. Then, on the inside of the plate, write out the message of 1 John 4:4:

"Greater is He that is living in me, than he that is in the world."

Measure and cut the length of string you'll need for your head, and tie the string to the two sides of the plate. Keep your superhero mask as a reminder that He is our superpower.

DISCUSSION QUESTIONS

Who is your favorite superhero? Why?

How can you call on God's Spirit when you're feeling weak?

Do you believe the Holy Spirit is stronger than any other power on Earth?

For through him God created everything in the heavenly realms and on earth. He made the things we can see and the things we can't see—such as thrones, kingdoms, rulers, and authorities in the unseen world. Everything was created through him and for him. He existed before anything else, and he holds all creation together.

Colossians 1:16–17 (NLT)

Better than an Octopus and *Stronger* than Glue

Have you ever wished you had an extra hand to help you hold on to something? Maybe when you were tidying up your toys or carrying a pile of freshly folded clothes that was about to topple over? It sure would be nice if you had extra hands in those tricky moments—like an octopus! Then you'd be able to hold lots of things.

Did you know that God is holding everything around us together? He is so amazing, yet invisible. All things have His fingerprints on them, from the birds and bees flying in the sky to the mountains and marvelous oceans. He has touched every fiber of our being. He created it all, and He's still holding it now. Do you know the song "He's Got the Whole World in His Hands"? It's a musical reminder that all we see (and don't see) is cradled within His care.

This is great news when we are feeling overwhelmed. Many times, we think we have to hold everything together by ourselves. But we only have two hands to work with! That's just not enough on those long, tough days. We feel exhausted and weary from the weight of everything we are trying to carry. But now, when we read these beautiful words of Paul, we are reminded that we aren't supposed to hold on to it all. We can share our heaviness and lighten our load when we come to our Father. Matthew 11:28 tells us that Jesus says, "*Come to me, all of you who are weary and carry heavy burdens, and I will give you rest.*" This is just another reminder of the power and strength that we can access.

We can also feel like things are unraveling quickly and coming apart, no matter how tightly we try to hold on to them. The truth is, we can go to God with those broken things, and He will fix them. So, when you feel overwhelmed and are having a terrible day, think of how we were created with only two hands, not eight. Even when things get heavy, we can still choose to lift them. After all, we have the assurance and knowledge that there is an invisible glue holding it all together—and that glue is your God. Trust Him with it all. His caring hands will cradle you.

PRAYER

Dear Heavenly Father,

We thank You for giving us rest. Help us come to You with our worries, troubles, and heavy things because when we talk to You, we can put it all down at Your feet. You want us to feel free so we may let it all go, knowing nothing is too heavy for You.

In Your name we pray,
Amen.

SUGGESTED ACTIVITY | God's Got This

Take a piece of paper and write down something troubling you in one color. Now, take another color, and underneath it, write the words, "God's got this." Hang your new artwork someplace you'll see every day this week, letting it remind you that He will help you with your burdens. He is in all things.

DISCUSSION QUESTIONS

What is something visible that God created? What is something invisible that God created?

What is the heaviest thing you can lift/hold?

What can God hold?

How can you find more rest this week? What can you hand over to Him, trusting that He is holding it?

Now when Jesus saw the crowds, he went up on a mountainside and sat down. His disciples came to him, and he began to teach them.

Matthew 5:1–2 (NIV)

WEEK 48

Don't Throw Away *the* Instructions!

Have you ever opened something cool, but then couldn't quite figure out how to make it work because—oops!—you threw away the instructions by mistake? You were probably so excited to start playing. The instructions are there to help you understand and use something properly. Sometimes, there's a long list of "how-to" instructions, which can take a long time to read through. However, if you ignore this step, you might accidentally break something or put it together wrong. It's worth taking the extra time and care to read up on how to best use your special new thing.

Did you know that Jesus gave us instructions on how to be our best? It's a long list, Matthew 5:1–12, entitled The Beatitudes. These directions are very important and come from God above. He's telling us what it's like to live the way He wants us to, using the phrase, "Blessed are ..." each time. So, grab your Bible, read Matthew 5:1–12, and then let's take a closer look!

1. ***"Blessed are the poor in spirit."*** This doesn't refer to the worldly poor; rather, it's talking about our need for a Savior. Joyful are those who know they need help and saving and look to God.
2. ***"Blessed are those who mourn."*** This refers to our sadness because of things we have done wrong, our sins. But we are holding onto hope. Joyful and comforted are those who know they are saved from their sins because of God's love.
3. ***"Blessed are the meek."*** The word "meek" refers to being gentle and practicing the fruit of the Spirit, self-control. Joyful are those who control their frustrations and actions.
4. ***"Blessed are those who hunger and thirst for righteousness."*** This refers to our urge to search for what is right. We know what it's like to be hungry and thirsty, and we understand the urge to satisfy that feeling. Joyful are those who want to know God more and seek His will and wisdom.

5. ***"Blessed are the merciful."*** This refers to the "Golden Rule." We all make mistakes and are in constant need of forgiveness. Thankfully, Jesus offers it to us daily, so we should offer it on to others. Joyful are those who are kind and forgiving.
6. ***"Blessed are the pure in heart."*** This refers to changing our hearts. It's easy to do the right thing when we get rewarded for it, but it's much harder to do it for the right reason—to please God. Joyful are those who work on their hearts and how they feel on the inside.
7. ***"Blessed are the peacemakers."*** This is a relatively easier one to understand. This refers to keeping the peace between people, which means standing up for what is right and not backing down and watching from the sidelines. Joyful are those who work to make peace.
8. ***"Blessed are those who are persecuted because of righteousness."*** This refers to when we speak or act on behalf of growing God's Kingdom and we're given hurtful words or angry actions. God sees this and considers our sacrifice. Joyful are those who suffer for God.
9. ***"Blessed are you when people insult you, persecute you, and falsely say all kinds of evil against you because of me."*** This is similar to number eight, but it goes on to say to rejoice and be glad because great is your reward.

God isn't trying to bore you. He is trying to build you. So, don't forget to read the instructions God has given us—the step-by-step details on how to live our best lives for Him.

PRAYER

Dear Heavenly Father,

We thank You for loving us so much that you gave us guidelines and rules to follow. These things will allow us to live in true happiness and joy, which is how You want our lives to be lived. Help us replace what the world says brings happiness with what You say brings us joy.

In Your name we pray,
Amen.

DISCUSSION QUESTIONS

Is it good to be a follower of the world? Or a follower of Jesus?

Good behavior is important to God. What can you work on this week that will bring Him and you more joy?

What is one thing Jesus taught in the Beatitudes that is different than everyone else's rules/ideas? How can you be "different" and try to be more like Jesus in attitude?

SUGGESTED ACTIVITY | "Blessed" Acrostic Poem

Make your own acrostic poem with the word "blessed." An acrostic poem uses each of the letters in the word, written on the left side of the paper from top to bottom. For example, the first letter of "blessed" is "b." You would try to come up with a word or phrase that begins with the letter "b." Then, move down a letter to the "l." What begins with that? Continue down the side of the paper with words or phrases that begin with each letter of your main word: "blessed." Try to tie each of the words or phrases into today's lesson!

Draw near to God, and he will draw near to you ...

James 4:8 (ESV)

WEEK 49

Giving God *Your* Crayon

In the adorable story *Harold and the Purple Crayon* by Crockett Johnson, curious little Harold creates his very own world with the power of his purple crayon. Around bedtime, he craves adventure, so he sets off for a walk. First, he wants to see the moon, so he simply draws it in the sky, and there it is. Next, he wants to follow a path. Using his imagination, he puts his purple crayon to good work and draws a path. From castles and dragons to sinking sailboats—whatever comes to Harold's mind, he brings to life through his magical crayon.

A good takeaway from this story is that Harold is in complete control of his life. Whatever he wants, he gets. Now, our lives are certainly not like that, but let's imagine they were. If you had a magical crayon, what kind of things would you create? Would you draw things for other people? Or just make things that your heart desires? What if you heard a heavenly voice asking to hold that crayon for you? Would you grip it tightly or let it go?

The verse from James speaks of how God greatly desires to grow close to you. But it starts with our desire to grow close to Him. When we are in His presence, we can freely hand over control. You see, this magical crayon may bring you your heart's desires, but God knows what is best for you. The more time you spend with Him, the more you'll want what He desires for you. James 4:6 states, "... *Therefore it says, 'God opposes the proud but gives grace to the humble.'*" To be proud means trying to do it all by ourselves. To be humble means we have surrendered our lives to God and have told Him that we need Him.

At the end of a Godly version of *Harold and the Purple Crayon*, Harold wouldn't just let his purple crayon fall out of his weary hand before going to sleep. Instead, before nodding off, a humble Harold would purposely place the crayon into the hands of the One who made the universe. After all the adventures Harold created on his own, he would finally realize that the best ones happen when God is the illustrator.

PRAYER

Dear Heavenly Father,

We thank You for the gift of life. You are the ultimate artist, bringing beautiful colors and pictures to us every day. When we feel the urge to take back the crayon from You, give us the wisdom and peace to know that when You are in control, our lives are better than we could ever draw by ourselves.

In Your name we pray,
Amen.

SUGGESTED ACTIVITY | Escape the Maze

Grab a bandana or scarf to use as a makeshift blindfold. Before you start, clear out a space in your house or yard and set up a simple "maze" using available household items. Working as a group or in pairs, designate one person to be the maze walker and one person to be the direction giver. Take the maze walker to the starting point and tie on the blindfold. Have their teammate give them clear directions to help them safely reach the end of the maze. Take turns until everyone has had a chance to be both the maze walker and the direction giver. Once done, discuss how it can be difficult to put your trust in God, but we can find peace knowing that He is in complete control of our lives and the directions they take.

DISCUSSION QUESTIONS

If you had a magical crayon, what would you draw?

Can you think of something you can give up to God?

Is it sometimes hard to completely trust God with the next steps and decisions in your life? Why?

All Scripture is God-breathed and is useful for teaching, rebuking, correcting and training in righteousness, so that the servant of God may be thoroughly equipped for every good work.

2 Timothy 3:16–17 (NIV)

WEEK 50

Don't Leave It *on the* Shelf!

Do you have a stuffed animal that you take everywhere? Maybe its eyes are not as bright, its fur not as fluffy, and its stuffing not as squishy as that of your other stuffed animals. That means you've loved that animal so much that it's not spending much time on a shelf—in fact, it's lost all the qualities it had when it was brand new. And that's okay! In fact, in the famous story *The Velveteen Rabbit* by Margery Williams, the rabbit learns that being used and loved by a child is the most important thing a stuffed animal can experience.

God also gave us something that He hopes we will love with all our might and take with us everywhere. It is His Word. Within the pages of the Bible lies the breath of God, "teaching" and "training" us day in and day out. Why? *"... so that the servant of God may be thoroughly equipped for every good work."* "Equipped" means ready and prepared, which is how our Heavenly Father wants us to feel with each footstep we take. There truly is a Bible verse for every occasion and decision we face. We just need to dig through those pages, find them, and use them.

A well-loved Bible might have marks, scribbles, circles, underlines, and pages folded over. And that's okay! That is what God wants for you: to carry His Word with you and to refer to it for wisdom. Sometimes, the way God tells us to live our lives conflicts with the messages of the world. But remember that He is on a mission to put you on the right path. He hopes you will also learn to love His guidance and messages.

"Fix these words of mine in your hearts and minds; tie them as symbols on your hands and bind them on your foreheads" (Deuteronomy 11:18).

What would it look like to have God's Word "*in your hearts and minds*"? It might look a little like a well-loved stuffed animal. So, grab that Bible off the shelf and pick up a bookmark and a bold-colored highlighter. It's time to use what you've been given!

PRAYER

Dear Heavenly Father,

Thank You for breathing new life into the pages of my Bible. Help me to care for it like a well-loved toy. Let me be inspired and strengthened by diving into Your Word daily.

In Your name we pray,
Amen.

SUGGESTED ACTIVITY | Bible Verse Scavenger Hunt

Grab a Bible or pull up an online Bible database. Taking turns, have each family member locate one of the verses below and fill in the missing word(s). Once done, discuss which are your favorite verses and why. **Recommended Bible version: NIV.*

- Psalm 56:3: *"When I am afraid, I put my _____ in you."*
- Philippians 4:13: *"I can do all this through Him who gives me _________."*
- Psalm 139:14: *"I praise you because I am _________ and __________ made."*
- 1 John 4:19: *"We ____ because He first _____ us."*
- Joshua 1:9: *"Have I not commanded you? Be strong and courageous. Do not be ______; do not be discouraged, for the LORD your God will be ____ ___ wherever you go."*
- Colossians 3:2: *"Set your mind on things _____, not on _______ things."*
- Romans 3:23: *"For all have _____ and fall short of the ____ of God."*
- Psalm 119:105: *"Your word is a ____ for my feet, a _____ on my path."*

DISCUSSION QUESTIONS

Which of your toys is looking a little worn?

What is something that goes everywhere with you?

How often do you open and read your Bible?

How can you make time this week to gather more wisdom from the Bible?

Remain in me, as I also remain in you. No branch can bear fruit by itself; it must remain in the vine. Neither can you bear fruit unless you remain in me. I am the vine; you are the branches. If you remain in me and I in you, you will bear much fruit; apart from me, you can do nothing.

John 15:4–5

WEEK 51

Staying *Connected*

There's a very fun version of the game of tag called "Blob Tag." Its rules are similar to the original game of tag, where you have to run around, trying not to get caught. The difference is that once you are tagged, you link up with the tagger to form a "blob." With more people running around, the aim is to stay connected. This is always funny to watch because some friends in the blob will want to go in one direction while others will try to go in another. It's hard to stay attached, especially when you're running around after people and trying to catch them, but it's the most important rule of the game.

There's also power in being connected, and Jesus knew this, too. To reinforce the message of togetherness, He uses the imagery of a grapevine because He knew it could be understood by those listening. In His time, many people grew grapes for wine, so they could picture the vine as He spoke. He told everyone how important it is to stay connected, using the image of Him as the vine and the listeners as the branches. It makes sense. After all, the branches must remain attached to the vine or else nothing will grow.

Jesus is speaking about relationships. When someone is important to you, it's good to spend time with them. But doing that takes work! You need to reach out and stay connected. God wants that same relationship with you. He wants you to be a part of Him so that He can be a part of you. When that connection is made, "*fruit*" can grow. By "*fruit*," He doesn't mean grapes and berries but the good things you do because of the good things He is doing in you. Without Him in our lives, our efforts run dry, and we "*can do nothing*." The passage goes on to say, "*If you do not remain in me, you are like a branch that is thrown away and withers; such branches are picked up, thrown into the fire and burned. If you remain in me and my words remain in you, ask whatever you wish, and it will be done for you*" (15:6–7).

So, the choice is ours! Will we remain, or exist, by reaching out to our sturdy vine, the One who can provide all we need and be full of fruit and fulfillment? Or will we "wither" because we didn't stay connected to God? Let your life overflow with the goodness and growth that only God can bring.

PRAYER

Dear Heavenly Father,

We thank You for reaching out to us. We know that without You, our lives would be dull and dry. But with You, so much can be accomplished. Please prune the areas of our lives where Your fruit isn't growing. We want to be full of life and full of Your goodness.

In Your name we pray,
Amen.

SUGGESTED ACTIVITY | Act It Out

Reread John 15:6–7 aloud, completing the corresponding actions:

- "I am the vine"—Move your arms around in the air.
- "You are the branches"—Stand as still as a tree with your hands up.
- "If you remain in me and I in you"—Hug your arms around your body.
- "You will bear much fruit"—Pretend you're picking fruit off a tree.
- "Apart from me, you can do nothing"—Hold your arms apart with your palms out.

DISCUSSION QUESTIONS

What fruits grow on branches?

What do you think happens to those fruits if the branches break?

What things can cause you to feel disconnected from God? How can you work on growing closer to Him this week?

For if you keep silent at this time, relief and deliverance will rise for the Jews from another place, but you and your father's house will perish. And who knows whether you have not come to the kingdom for such a time as this?

Esther 4:14 (ESV)

WEEK 52

The *Best* Spoiler Alert

Has anyone ever told you the ending of a book you were reading or ruined the last scene of a movie you couldn't wait to watch? Maybe someone has jumped in and told the punchline to a joke you were about to share. It's such a spoiler! However, what if you knew the ending to something that was troubling you, and it gave you great hope?

This is the bold truth that you can grab hold of when you follow God. He goes before you and has great plans for you, so you can rest assured knowing the ending: whatever comes your way, God is with you and will give you what you need.

This week's passage is from a conversation between Queen Esther and her cousin, Mordecai. He was begging her to go to the king, her husband, on behalf of all the Jewish people, to save their lives. But there was one problem: no one could go before the king, not even his wife, unless they had been asked to do so. By approaching him with such a huge request, she was risking her own life. So, she asked her cousin and all the Jewish people to pray for the strength and courage to do what was needed. "*And who knows whether you have not come to the kingdom for such a time as this?*" Mordecai's bold question helped her to focus on the thoughtful plans of God and remove her fear. God placed Esther in the right place at the right time to do His work. And He is doing the same for you.

Whether it is a difficult decision or a path that needs your patience, you can persevere and face the challenge head-on because God has put you in that position to do His will. He won't ask you to do it alone. Matthew 28:20 can give you hope for every situation: "*... And surely I am with you always, to the very end of the age*" (NIV). Focus on each of those words; they are bold and courageous, just like you can be. You don't need to know every detail of your life to know how the story ends because if your author is God—spoiler alert—the last words are always "in victory."

PRAYER

Dear Heavenly Father,

We thank You for creating us for times like these. Help us to lean into Your handiwork and trust our part in it. Whether we are having a quick conversation with a neighbor, starting a new friendship, or moving house, You are always at work. Even when we cannot see how it all will end, give us Your eternal hope so that we can shine brightly into this world wherever we are.

In Your name we pray,
Amen.

SUGGESTED ACTIVITY | Faith over Fear

Give each family member a piece of paper and fold it in half. On the inside, write down some of your fears. On the outside, write the word "faith." Around the table, reflect upon and discuss how having faith can help you overcome these fears.

DISCUSSION QUESTIONS

Can you think of a time when you had to be strong and courageous?

Read chapter 4 of Esther together as a family. What was Esther's bigger purpose in this story?

Do you think God sometimes allows troubles into our lives so that we are driven toward Him? If so, what can you learn through the experience?

Acknowledgments

To my Heavenly Maker, for lovingly guiding my heart and my hands.

To my husband, who steadily fed me coffee as I wrote in the early hours of the morning and watched and bathed the babies as I continued typing through dinner and into the hours of the night. Thank you for your never-ending support of my writing dreams. I love you.

To my beautiful band of daughters, thank you for cheering me on, for listening after I wrote each paragraph, for the constructive feedback on word choices and activities, and for just being my biggest supporters. I love you all so very much!

To my parents, for constant and prayerful support in chasing dreams rooted in God's gifts. I cannot wait to sit on the couch and read these pages with you both by my side. Thank you for inspiring me through your love and wisdom.

To my wonderful brother and sister, who never cease to cheer me on in every adventure.

To my friend Becky, who continually offered words of encouragement when I was starting off, completely stuck, or finally finished!

To my faithful friend Emily, who served me caffeine and cookies while stocking me with verses! I'm so grateful for your friendship and unwavering faith.

To my Walking with Purpose warriors and those at St. Mary's, for preparing me with Bible verses and bringing a passion for God's love story into my daily life. And for praying through this exciting journey!

To my amazing editors, Olivia and Lindsay, for believing in my writing and approaching me with this wonderful family concept. I have felt so blessed through this whole project and can't thank you enough for partnering with me.

To the whole Paige Tate & Co. team, for putting together this beautiful book to help families to grow together in God's amazing Word.

About the Author

Monica Stoltzfus is an avid crafter, composer of words, coffee addict, and chaos wrangler. Her debut picture book, *The Ripple*, was awarded first place by the National Indie Excellence Awards for "Best Inspirational Children's Book." Her second book, *Just Compose Yourself: Finding Hope in Spilled Coffee*, is a collection of stories to help lift and look up when things feel down. When not writing, she can be found watching a Hallmark movie marathon, shopping at craft stores, or spending time with friends and her Bible. She lives in Northern Virginia with her five fearless daughters and compassionate husband. To stay updated on her journey of crafting creations, motherhood mayhem, and faith-filled stories, check out her blog, www.justcomposeyourself.com.